LICENSED
TO
PROFIT

LICENSED
TO
PROFIT

by Trading in Financial Markets

Chris Shea

Wrightbooks

BICENTENNIAL
1807
WILEY
2007
BICENTENNIAL

First published in 2007 by Wrightbooks
an imprint of John Wiley & Sons Australia, Ltd
42 McDougall Street, Milton Qld 4064

Office also in Melbourne

Typeset in Berkeley LT 11.2/14 pt

© Chris Shea 2007

The moral rights of the author have been asserted

National Library of Australia Cataloguing-in-Publication data:

Shea, Chris

Licensed to profit: by trading in financial markets.

Includes index.

ISBN 9780731406838 (pbk.).

1. Stocks. 2. Investments. 3. Speculation. I. Title.

332.6322

Front cover © Corbis Corporation and John Kelly/Getty Images

Wiley bicentennial logo: Richard J Pacifico

Printed in Australia by McPherson's Printing Group

10 9 8 7 6 5 4 3 2 1

Disclaimer

The material in this publication is of the nature of general comment only, and does not represent professional advice. It is not intended to provide specific guidance for particular circumstances and it should not be relied on as the basis for any decision to take action or not take action on any matter which it covers. Readers should obtain professional advice where appropriate, before making any such decision. To the maximum extent permitted by law, the author and publisher disclaim all responsibility and liability to any person, arising directly or indirectly from any person taking or not taking action based upon the information in this publication.

Contents

About the author

Chris Shea is a trader, educator and psychotherapist who specialises in coaching those who want to become and stay successful in financial markets. He assists clients to sustain superior returns by helping them discover and use their own approach based on their unique personality and talent.

Chris has an established track record in coaching clients to develop the skills and drive to become independent, disciplined and very profitable traders. Coaching SuperTraders is his forte.

He is a founding shareholder of Automated Trading Solutions PL, and holds a bachelor of education and a master of science, as well as a diploma of professional counselling.

While based in Brisbane, Chris has private and institutional clients in all states of Australia, New Zealand, Los Angeles and Singapore.

Visit <www.themarketcoach.com> for more information.

Introduction

It's generally believed that most people who intend to trade in financial markets don't succeed. That is, most people do not profit from the financial markets. Rather, they forfeit part or all their trading capital, and then move on to other life projects with feelings of bitterness and betrayal about their market experience. The conventional wisdom is that about 70 per cent of market entrants end up in this category.

By my estimate, a further 20 per cent of traders have advanced to the extent that they are in what I call the 'break-even rut': their results are variable, neither consistently winning nor losing.

The remaining 10 per cent are the consistent winners. These market players have an edge that enables them to operate a highly profitable risk management business in financial markets.

In my professional life as a trading coach I have helped hundreds of traders all over the world to join the top 10 per cent. How do I do it? That's what I've set out to explain in this book, taking a simple, step-by-step approach aimed at giving you all the tools you'll need to become one of that 10 per cent.

Getting into the Zone—learning to drive

I call my clients who achieve outstanding profits 'SuperTraders', and I encourage all my clients to envision themselves as potential SuperTraders. SuperTraders operate in the 'Peak Performance Zone', achieving outstanding profits.

The Zone is the sweet spot that is experienced by top professionals in any field. Think of Tiger Woods winning a string of majors, an opera singer giving a virtuoso recital, or a surgeon doing open heart surgery.

The Zone is not an exclusive club. You will have experienced being in the Zone many times in your life. This is when you have practiced a skill so much that it becomes second nature, for example when you are driving your car. When you drive, you execute the actions required by the road conditions and the traffic (the information flow), moment by moment. When you drive your car well you are functioning flawlessly, beyond cognition. You don't calculate the velocity difference or relative kinetic energy between you and the vehicle you are overtaking. You just do it. That's the Zone.

Or, to put it another way, you are unconsciously working competently in a super-conscious state: the Zone. The term SuperTrader relates to working in a similar super-conscious state, this time in the trading environment.

Driving a car is far more dangerous than trading. Every time you take the car on the road you put your life at risk. But this does not inhibit good performance; rather it enhances it. It's a must that you operate in the Zone without fear and anxiety but with the very positive expectation that you will achieve your destination.

To trade with consistent profitability it's a must that you operate in exactly the same way: without fear and anxiety, but with positive expectations. Additionally, you must be up to responding intelligently, skilfully and spontaneously to the market 'traffic'.

To achieve the consistency and trading success that being in the Zone affords, I ask my clients to look at all four elements of the Zone. Each is an attribute that you have. To operate in the Zone, you need to ensure that each of these four elements within you is functioning at a high level.

The first is physiological. Doesn't it make sense that you will achieve better outcomes if your physiology allows you to operate in a powerful state of relaxed yet alert centeredness, rather than with adrenalin shock and the fight/flight impulse whenever you encounter stress?

The emotional element addresses the fear and anxiety associated with trading. You don't know the future in a market; anything can happen. Fear and anxiety are natural emotions in this setting, but it's important to be able to recognise these emotions and not allow yourself to be governed by them. Self-worth and knowing what you are doing go a long way to countering irrational fears. When you are feeling calmness, self-belief, and optimism, you will be functioning in the right emotional space to be in the Zone.

The Zone has an intellectual element. You have to know what you are doing. Are you gambling or running a profitable risk management business? Do you know that your trading strategy is resourceful and resilient enough to produce the outcomes you desire? Have you accessed the full repertoire of intellectual skills — believe it or not, there are eight or nine distinct skills — to improve your intellectual edge?

Action is the fourth and most important element of the Zone. You need to practise integrating your positive physiology and emotions with your strategy, so that you execute your trades intuitively and flawlessly. In practice, this means beginning initially with a small account size, performing deliberately and mechanically. With enough practice and appropriate feedback, you will develop the perception and precision to execute your strategy automatically. This takes time and perseverance — however the results are well and truly worth it.

Practice makes perfect

Research from the University of Sydney and the Westmead Hospital Brain Research Unit reveals that to fully learn a new skill, you will have to repeat the action up to 1000 times.

Think about when you first learned to drive a car. Remember how you mastered the four elements of the Zone over time, rather than all at once? At first you had to deliberately think: to start off in first gear, you need to let the clutch out a little, while simultaneously depressing the accelerator. When the car starts to move, then you let the clutch out quickly and entirely with more acceleration. It wasn't that easy, right? And not only this, but you also had to be aware of other matters: Is the road ahead clear? What is the traffic behind you doing? What should your next manoeuvre be?

And so it goes. You continuously practise the new skills of driving under instruction until you present for your driving test. If you prove that you are competent against a standard set of criteria in a driving test then you'll receive your driver's licence. If you fail the test you can have another go, until eventually you pass.

It's not until you have your licence that you can really perfect your new skills through the experience of driving on your own, in different road conditions and situations. In other words, your licence proves you are 'consciously competent'; you can then advance with continual practice to the unconscious driving Zone.

Learning to drive a car is a much more complex and dangerous activity than learning to trade. Yet almost all who want to learn to drive succeed in their aim. It begs the question: If 99 per cent of learners can learn to drive a car well enough to gain their licence, then why is it that only 10 per cent of people succeed at trading?

The answer lies in the fact that most who attempt to trade never actually learn the skills of trading under instruction. Most never secure their licence to trade profitably. They expect the impossible: to start in the Zone.

Let me give you an example to illustrate my point. A heart surgeon does not start out doing open heart surgery at the beginning of her career. First she must study and be tested to receive a licence to be a doctor. As she advances from intern to resident to registrar to consultant in her area, her talent and skills develop. After years of study and examination, she can perform as surgeon. Years of practice and discipline have allowed her to perform confidently, consistently and flawlessly in the Zone. Rest assured her patients are thankful that she has achieved the heart surgery Zone. Yet most novice traders expect to acquire the heart surgeon income without even obtaining the initial trading licence.

I'll put it another way. Would you allow a first-time driver to go onto a busy six-lane freeway alone without first obtaining a licence? Your answer is obviously 'no'.

Yet this is what most novices do in trading. To extend the metaphor, the novice trader goes to the showroom where the software or systems salesperson sells the dream of freedom and persuades the novice to exchange hard-won capital for a shiny new trading car. The trader is given some analysis (let's call it a road map) and is then expected to drive it away without practising any trading skills or securing the licence to drive. Little wonder that most people crash their trading car—and their dreams—before they develop the expertise to drive.

Whether you're a novice needing the basics or you're stuck in the break-even rut, this book aims to help you move on and into the Zone.

Preparing to obtain your licence to trade is a vital step in your transformation to becoming profitable and remaining permanently in the Zone. This book aims to fill the gap that your software and trading platform can't provide. Its purpose is to enable you to take advantage of analytical techniques that present high probability set-ups.

In this book I'll give you the trading 'road' rules and explain why you need to stick to these rules for safety. *Licensed to Profit* presents you with the full repertoire of skills needed to drive (and get the most out of) your trading 'car'.

Licensed to Profit teaches you the necessity of practising these skills so you can become a competent, profitable trader.

I'll also deal with some potential hurdles, especially with respect to your own negative self-talk, which needs to be overcome to allow efficient practice. Finally I'll present your driving licence test. It sets out the standard set of criteria that you must achieve before you can be awarded your trading licence.

Once you have your trading licence you will have confirmed that you are at the threshold of the top 10 per cent. From then on you have the choice to successfully drive your trading car to wherever you will, if you are prepared to work towards it and the SuperTrader Zone. I'm not saying it's easy—just like learning to drive, it requires hard work—and of course you are risking the possibility of failure. But in my opinion if you have made the effort to learn to drive a car well then you can make the same effort to learn to trade well, and profitably—if it is your will and passion.

Can you secure your trading licence, progress to the trading Peak Performance Zone and reap the consequent rewards? I think so, if you are committed to practice and improvement. In trading, as with all walks of life, the Peak Performance Zone enables ordinary people to achieve extraordinary outcomes.

Your licence to trade positions you for success

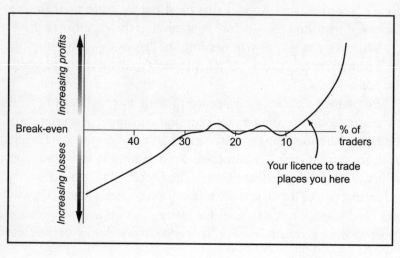

Developing road sense: what's trading all about?

Everyone who attempts to drive a car expects to succeed at it. From an early age, each of us has witnessed competent driving skills, watching family members and others on the roads. It's just part of our social context. What we observe as a youngster is that driving is a continuous process of awareness and actions which require focus and purpose. And so before we learn to drive ourselves, we already have a model of what driving is all about.

Our experience shows us that the capacity to drive is independent of intellectual capacity and social status. Attaining a driver's licence indicates motivation and persistence, a willingness to learn the processes of competent driving. For young adults, obtaining a drivers' licence is a rite of passage into freedom and responsibility.

But do you know what? There is no gene for driving ability. Your great-great-grandparents were restricted to horse and buggy—no automobiles for them! In fact, 125 years ago, vehicles exceeding speeds of 10 kph needed a red warning flag. Your ancestors would be both frightened and amazed that you can hurtle down the freeway at 110 kph. Your journey to and from the shopping centre takes you minutes. For them, it would have taken a day.

Just imagine putting your great-great-grandparents into a car today and expecting them to drive it. They couldn't do it! Although they are genetically similar to you, they lack the experience and learning to just hop in the car and drive it away safety and competently. Nevertheless given the same training and experience as you, they could certainly manage to drive well.

Why trading is like driving a car

Driving a car is a learned behaviour that operates within a social context: other road users. Similarly, trading is a learned behaviour within a social context: the market.

Just as for driving, there is no gene for trading. Think of your poor old great-great-grandparents in the car for the first time. Unless you come from a family or social group that is successful at trading then you really are in the same position as your forebears. You will exhibit the same qualities of fear and amazement; and you will lack the experience and understanding that enable success.

Processes rather than outcomes

Like driving, trading is a learned behaviour. In order to trade successfully, you first need a model of the processes that lead to competence and success in trading. Then, you need to practise them with motivation and persistence in order to achieve your licence — or in this case, your ability to trade well.

Just like your great-great-grandparents, you can learn the processes that will make you successful.

How do markets pay you?

One of the best ways I know of for a newcomer to understand a market is to witness a market process which is easily accessible and understandable: I recommend you go to a house auction.

The vendor of the house doesn't want it anymore, for whatever reason, so she puts it up for sale at auction. Of course she doesn't want to give it away, so she establishes a reserve with the auctioneer beforehand. Let's say the reserve is $1 million. The vendor won't release the house for any price below this figure. Instead, she hopes that the reserve is at least met. What she is *really* hoping for, though, is that someone wants the house so much that he is prepared to pay more than $1 million for it.

If the auctioneer has done a good job of publicising the auction, when the day comes there should be quite a large crowd in attendance. Only one person in the crowd will actually buy the house, and then only if his bid is the highest above $1 million.

Of the 20 or 30 people present, most will be spectators. They are neighbours interested in the sale price relative to their own home, people gauging the state of the house market, supporters of the vendor, or even people who just enjoy witnessing the drama of the auction process.

Typically, only a few people in the crowd are genuinely prepared to bid. They actually want the house. They have an idea of what it is worth to them, and know what they are prepared to pay. They understand that once their bid is made it becomes a binding commitment.

The auctioneer starts the bidding at $880000. At this stage the vendor—although she knows the reserve—may feel shocked that her home is unappreciated. Slowly the bidders, reluctant to show their hand, and not wanting to jack the price up against themselves, reveal their hand. $900000, $925000, $950000, $975000, $1 million is bid. Now look at the vendor. What a relief! Her home is appreciated and she is now in profit. What she won't do is say to the auctioneer, 'Stop the auction. That's enough for me.' Not at all. Now she is in the wonderful position of letting the remaining serious buyers duel it out.

The next bid is $1.050 million. It's really hotting up. $1.100 million, $1.175 million, $1.250 million, $1.310 million, $1.335 million, and lastly $1.350 million: the house is sold at $1.350 million.

For the new owner to make a profit, he must sell the house for a price in excess of his purchase price. But the auction process tells him that since his was the highest bid he will have to wait or do some

3

work on the house before he can sell it for profit. The price he could immediately sell it for is $1.335 million, the price of the bid just before his final bid, assuming that potential buyer is still interested. If approached too soon, the second-last bidder would appreciate the buyer's distress and most likely drastically lower the price at which he would be prepared to buy.

Figure 1.1: bids at a house auction

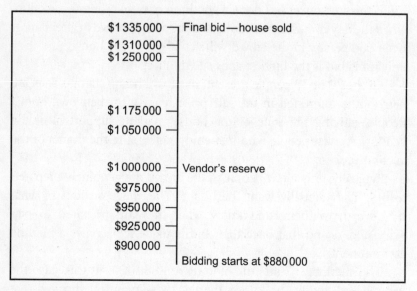

$1 335 000 — Final bid—house sold
$1 310 000
$1 250 000

$1 175 000
$1 050 000

$1 000 000 — Vendor's reserve
$975 000
$950 000
$925 000
$900 000
Bidding starts at $880 000

That's how an auction market works. As prices appreciate, vendors keep their hands in their pockets and let the prices flow upwards until the last buyer is standing. Conversely, when prices are declining, vendors must take what they can get because in this case the buyers have their hands in their pockets until the last seller has sold.

Markets work because the buyer and the vendor, counterparties to the deal, have completely opposing views. The buyer looking for profit says: 'Prices must go up after I buy', while the vendor says: 'The price will decline after I sell'. Only one of them can be right.

Active financial markets are continuous and vigorous auctions with many participants, as well as watchers. Although there are many players, the price at any moment in time is set by only two participants: the buyer and seller at that price. This price then becomes information for the next deal, and the next and so on. The net effect is that markets go up, down or sideways according to the perceptions and actions of buyers and sellers who are attempting to make a profit.

So the house auction market works upwards in price without a deal being completed until the final price is reached. The financial market, on the other hand, represents a continuous flow of completed deals. For example, using the auction prices from above, you would see a flow of completed deals at all prices from $880 000 to $1.350 million. Unlike in the auction, there are plenty of players who are prepared to deal at $901 000, $902 000 and $903 000. They can profit if the price appreciated for a few points; or, as sellers, they can profit if the price depreciates by a few points. If they successfully repeat this many times then their profits will be substantial. We call these players 'jobbers' or 'intraday traders'. They fill in the gaps in the price movement, and in so doing make the market continuous.

But what about the person who buys at around $900 000 and sells around $1.300 million? These people are called 'position' or 'trend' traders. These traders do not dip in and out repeatedly but instead take a longer term approach.

There is a huge advantage in the financial market that is unavailable to those buying or selling houses. When you buy a house, you have to buy the entire thing all at once. This is not the case in the financial market. At $900 000 you might buy the equivalent of the kitchen. If the prices don't rise and you have to sell at $880 000, you only lose 20 points on only the kitchen, and even better, you haven't spent $1.350 million on the whole house—just $900 000. But if prices do go from $900 000 to $1.350 million then you could add the lounge room at $912 000, the bedrooms at $925 000 and $940 000, and the rest of the house at $950 000. Furthermore as the prices approached $1.300 million you might start selling off portions of the house to lock in profit, as the price seems to be becoming exorbitant. And what happens if prices start to plummet? At this point, you do not want to own any part of the house. Whether you still own the whole house or only part of it at this stage, as a trader you must sell it.

So how do markets pay you? It's pretty simple really. You get paid by agreeing with the direction of the price movement in the market. You get paid by being in sync with the market direction. By buying, you are assuming that prices will climb after you buy—buying is a bet that prices will go up. If they do go up, then the market will pay you as long as it continues to go up. Of course the market won't go up just because you think it will or because you have just bought. (By the way, market jargon for entering a purchase is going 'long' in the market.)

If the market goes down after you buy, you pay. Conversely, it is possible to profit from a falling market by selling a position and retaining it as long as the market declines. (Market jargon for entering a sale is going 'short' on the market.)

Most importantly, the market cannot pay you at all if you don't have a position. You can't profit by being a spectator.

In summary, if you have bought you will profit if the market subsequently goes up. If you have sold you profit if the market falls. The market *must* pay you as long as you are in harmony with it. If you're not in harmony with the market, you pay. Obviously the best thing to do is to get in harmony with the market flow.

Speculation: betting on the future

Visualise yourself driving on a country highway. You have been following a slow vehicle around a series of bends. You can't overtake at the moment although that's what you would like to do. Eventually, a straight appears and you perceive that you have enough clear road ahead to safety pass the slow vehicle. That perception is a speculation upon which you can now act.

Because it is a speculation rather than a certainty, it doesn't mean that you can't act on it. The road is clear now but you can't be certain that it will remain so. There is a risk involved. However you decide not to wait until the next bend to see if another vehicle is indeed heading towards you. You take the risk now and remain vigilant.

As you begin to pass the slow car, you stay alert. Moment by moment you're prepared to alter your action as required. In fact your mind is constantly scanning the road ahead to confirm that your speculation that it's safe to pass still holds. You identify and manage the risk using your driving skill and experience. You do not hesitate to take the opportunity, although there is no rule or guarantee that ensures your safe passage around the slow vehicle. Anything could happen. While you would prefer a smooth run, a car could come around the corner towards you, the vehicle you are overtaking could speed up, a tyre could blow out, or another vehicle could turn in from a side road.

Figure 1.2: delay is counterproductive

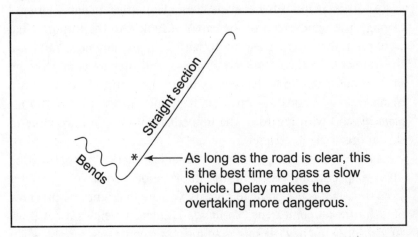

As long as the road is clear, this is the best time to pass a slow vehicle. Delay makes the overtaking more dangerous.

All being well, though, you pass the slow vehicle smoothly and successfully. Whatever happens, you are responsive and adjust to any new circumstance. Although you may not be in control of the external circumstances—other cars and so on—you are in control of your own actions, decisions and responses. You continuously manage the process of overtaking.

What you were doing is speculating that you would successfully overtake the slow vehicle. But this speculation is only appropriate to one specific moment in time. You didn't assume that the road *must* remain clear before you. You could not afford to rigidly hold that view. If a car did come towards you while overtaking, you would not allow your vehicle to crash into it. You would hit the brakes, let it pass and take the next opportunity to overtake. Once you commenced overtaking the slow vehicle you were fully engaged and committed to dealing with whatever situation arose. The speculation was just the beginning of a series of actions, and if the circumstances alter, so, consequently, will your speculations.

Let me present you with another driving and trading analogy. You are driving on a city arterial road. You have a green light, so you go. The next set of lights goes red just as you approach them. Do you drive straight through it because you believe that you're entitled to a clear run with only green lights? Of course not! You stop. If you do not drive according to the traffic conditions, the ultimate outcome is that you will crash.

Another point can be made here. You drive looking forward through the windscreen of the car. You look into the future. What went on in the past is irrelevant to what is happening now. You leave the last set of traffic lights, red or green, and prepare yourself to go or stop depending on what comes up in the future. In driving you manage your actions not on what happened in the past but *in the moment*, and with regard to the immediate future. I'll have more to say on this topic in chapter 3.

When you enter a position in a financial market, you are acting upon a speculation based on the information you have right now. Even though it is not polite to say this, you are in essence betting now on a future outcome. The *Macquarie Dictionary* defines a bet thus: 'to risk one's money'. It might sound crass, but, put simply, when you trade you are betting with some of your capital on a particular outcome in the future.

In financial markets, as in driving a car, anything can happen at any time.

When you initiate a position, that is, enter the market, it can only ever be a speculation since you, or anybody else for that matter, cannot know the future.

Remember you will profit if the market goes up after you buy. The act of buying implies this hope. But once the position is entered you have to drive your trade with the same degree of responsiveness and flexibility with which you drive a car in relation to the other traffic on the road. This means that if you buy a position to go up, but it goes down, you've experienced something equivalent to a red light, and you must stop. In practice, you would exit the position. In other words, if your bet is wrong, get out.

If you don't drive your trade in a businesslike and professional way, with discipline and detached respect, you are likely to crash. Part of that discipline is being realistic and rational about speculation.

By realising that you are speculating now about a future outcome, it frees you up from what happened in the past and from having rigid views of how the future must unfold.

The business of financial speculation

It may seem strange that I need to remind you that speculation in financial markets—either through active investing or trading—is a business. But it's surprising how many people don't see it that way.

An arbitrary and unsystematic 'hit or miss' approach is little more than gambling. Even if it is spasmodically successful, it will not provide sustainable returns in the long run. One very real danger of intermittent returns is that it can reinforce the gambling instinct and give the illusion of success. After all, poker machines are designed to provide some return, with the possibility of a very large but rare return keeping the punters interested. Although the odds are well and truly against them, chasing those intermittent returns can prove addictive to some.

The outcome of speculation does not rely on luck. The whole enterprise must be approached with insight, wisdom and professionalism.

How do the financial markets compare with other businesses?

The goal of any business is to be profitable, and for those profits to be sustainable and growing. I can hear your wry comment that this is just stating the obvious: everybody knows the aim of business is to stay in business. So why do so many fail in the business of speculation in financial markets?

One reason for failure is that a businesslike approach may not be employed. If you go into this project saying to yourself 'I can afford to lose $20 000', then you probably will.

Speculation is a challenging business, but no more so than others, especially in the start-up stage. Most start-up enterprises fail, and fail within two years. The goal for a start-up business is to develop an edge that can be established into a franchise that can endure and expand over time. In other words, you need to secure your licence to prove you can profit—and *then* you can go on with it.

Establishment of your franchise in speculation is just like that in any other business. You have to develop and implement routines and procedures that cause success. You need to quantify, analyse and evaluate your edge. To make it worthwhile, you have to know that your activity leads to profits superior to other endeavours that you might engage in. If you don't develop a franchise then you can't plan to expand your business. If you aren't profitable then you don't have a business.

The business of speculation in financial markets offers lots of advantages over many other businesses. I've listed some of them below.

Financial markets are 'blind' in the sense that they are unconcerned about your gender, age, race, religion, sexual orientation, muscular strength, physical coordination, experience, expectations, hopes and dreams. The market's only concern is whether or not you have the resources to pay your margin and stand behind your bet. (When you drive your car out of your driveway you aren't concerned about the personal characteristics of the other drivers. Your only concern is that they have proven their competence by obtaining their driver's licence.)

Markets tell the truth the whole time. There are no information barriers in this job if you deal in active markets. Okay, a huge trading house can possibly cause a blip in the very short term but even so the recorded course of sales are facts available for all to see and can't be doctored or changed. In that sense the playing field is absolutely level. Winners and losers have the same information base.

The information upon which you base your decisions is very high grade. I'm talking here about the deal flow (the prices that are actually traded), not newspaper stories or gossip or tips or chatroom talk that surrounds the market. Looking at the deal flow, you don't have to distinguish spin or distortions. You just have to keep your eyes on the road.

In this business *skill and experience are everything.* You will not win just because you are a nice person or just because you turn up.

You are unable to charm or bully your way through the market as you might with employees, or in other forms of business. (As an aside—don't let your broker or software provider charm or bully you either.)

The reliability of the information means that *you know your bottom line at all times*. This business enables accurate and continuous record-keeping. You can always know your score instantaneously, with objectivity and without embellishment. (When you drive your car, you know exactly where you are in relation to your destination at all times.)

You do not need a great deal of capital to commence trading. I have clients who start with under $5000 per position; of course, there are others who trade over $500 000 at a time. If you can handle a small account successfully then you can quantify your franchise as a basis for increasing your trade size in the future. Doesn't this make sense? You have probably heard the old joke about the futures trader who won a million dollars in the lottery. When asked what he was going to do with this windfall he replied 'keep trading until it's all gone'. Needless to say his approach is not businesslike.

The plant and equipment required for speculation is minimal. You don't need to invest in a shop or factory. Your equipment list runs to no more than a fast computer, data, perhaps analysis software and a cable/satellite/broadband connection or phone line. You don't have employees and all the associated ramifications. Neither do you need a marketing budget.

What are the special features of the business of speculation?

The peculiarities of the business of speculation mean success in another business venture or profession will not automatically guarantee your success at this one. The most important aspect of this business is to accept and work with the reality that there is nothing you can do to alter the market outcome. Remember the person who bought the house for $1.350 million? He might have bought a residence as a property developer so that he could refurbish and remarket for a much higher price. *In financial markets, though, you cannot add value to your position.* But why would you bother? You don't need to. That's an advantage of the business, rather than a hindrance.

Remember if your ideas and consequent actions are in harmony with the market flow, then you will succeed. If they are out of kilter then your bet will lose. Markets will ruthlessly expose false beliefs, sharp practices and lack of ability. Put another way, the market imposes on speculators a discipline that if ignored will cause loss and potential ruin. Let me repeat with emphasis: *You will not succeed in this business without the appropriate discipline and routine.* Just like driving.

One of the hallmarks of the business of trading is timelines. You have to be prepared for the unusual and the unexpected. *You have to act promptly and decisively in the light of the information and your analysis of it.* In other business situations you can sit on information, and in fact it can pay to do so. (For example, a business might process all accounts once a month rather than as they come in, for efficiency.) Procrastination, seeking a second opinion, or forming a committee to investigate might pay off in other businesses; none of these delaying strategies work in speculation.

All business is a speculation about the future. As the old saying goes, 'You are only as good as your next customer'. Irrespective of how successful you have been in other business or even with speculation in financial markets in the past, if you reject or neglect market discipline then you will not succeed. *You are only as good as your next trade!* Of course this is true in driving, too. Although you may have an unblemished record as a driver, if you lose your concentration and do something silly and undisciplined, then you will come to grief.

Can the professional skills and discipline required for this business be learned? Yes, emphatically yes: in the same way you learn to drive a car. The aim of any professional education is to foster understanding, discipline and routine so that the practitioner can deal with the ordinary and the unusual in a premeditated and effective way. A commercial airline pilot, although licensed and experienced, regularly trains for the unexpected in the simulator to be prepared for any eventuality that might occur in the future.

Learning the skills, discipline and routines for this business does require commitment in terms of time, effort and practice. Unfortunately many are enticed into speculation with a superficial notion of what's actually required while still expecting instantaneous success, rather like the poker machine player. In a cynical way we could say these amateur players will contribute to your profits.

Why is it so difficult to win consistently?

As I've mentioned, there is a common belief that only 10 per cent of people who set out to become traders actually achieve their initial desire for consistent high returns over the long haul. Objective data to verify this belief would be extremely difficult to obtain in practical terms. In fact I haven't seen any hard data on it. However if we applied the Pareto principle to this belief, we would see that 20 per cent of the traders take 80 per cent of the money. Pareto, an Italian economist, formed the idea that 80 per cent of the consequences stem from 20 per cent of the causes, and this 80–20 rule is commonly accepted in business.

So then the question arises: why do a few win when most don't? Furthermore, what do the few who win big do that the crowd of non-winners doesn't do?

The techniques of winners

As a successful trading coach I have worked with clients in all parts of the trading success spectrum. Most of my work is with top professional and institutional trader clients, who profit by many hundreds of thousands, and some millions, a year. These are my 'SuperTraders'. Like top professionals in any field, coaching is very important to maintain and extend performance. SuperTraders go about their business from the perspective of speculation in a way that is different to the majority. Put simply, the SuperTrader identifies, accepts and manages (that is, trades) positions that represent no more than *conjectures* about the future. My *Concise Oxford Dictionary* defines conjecture as 'formation of an opinion on incomplete grounds, a guess'.

Now in dealing with the future we know one thing for sure: the future is unknowable. Anything can happen—from what you expect, to something completely unexpected. For example, an event could happen in the next instant that could change your life forever. You might receive news of an unexpected inheritance from a long-lost relative, or on the other hand you could hear some terrible news such as a loved one's involvement in a fatal accident. In life, though, most people don't dwell on this existential reality, and simply deal with issues as they arise.

However in the business of speculation, the trader must not only deal with the uncertainty of an unknowable future but also embrace it. Why is this so? Because taking positions of uncertainty involves risk. The speculator's return is directly proportional to the capacity to accept and manage risk.

Trading has an additional dimension. Unlike in life, in trading there is an active counterparty to your stance about the future. This counterparty backs the exact opposite to your view and requires you to pay up if you are wrong. (Of course, if your speculation is right, you get paid.) Take this example. The price of a security is currently $5.00. The speculator conjectures that the security may be worth $10.00 in the future and so buys. This conjecture is of necessity based on the extrapolation of very incomplete and tentative information, perhaps fundamental, and/or technical, or even intuitive. Nevertheless the position seems to contain a lot of risk because if the crowd thought the security was worth $10.00, then what would be its price now? Yes, that's right: $10.00. *So the speculator thinks and acts differently to the crowd.* A speculator's work is proactive and counterintuitive to the uninitiated.

It is apparent that the speculator who buys at $5.00 and sells at $10.00 profits more than those who bought at $6.00 or $7.00. At these prices, buyers are becoming more comfortable; buying seems safer and so the crowd begins to join in. You can see that *if you are part of the crowd then your opportunity for huge profits is diminished.*

The speculator acts before the crowd and seizes the opportunity without hesitation. (Remember: the best time to overtake a slow vehicle is at the beginning of the clear straight. You don't wait until the corner looms.) See figure 1.3.

Figure 1.3: speculator acts before the crowd

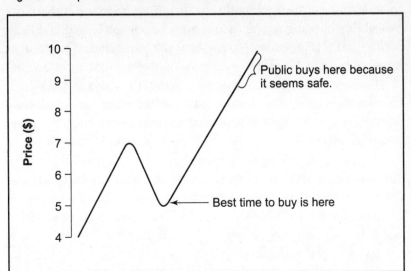

This means that the speculator buys when there is very little interest in the security. At this time, as far as other buyers are concerned, the security seems unsafe to buy. This is because there is scant information that confirms it will go to a much higher price. By the time the security seems safe to buy—because the information about the quality of the security has become available—everybody else will be buying. That is, of course, except for the speculators who are selling to them and doing very well out of it.

And what happens after the last person has bought? Yes, that's right: as we saw at the house auction, the market begins to plummet.

In essence, a speculator prefers to buy from distressed sellers and sell to panic buyers.

All this is another way of saying that speculative profit comes from buying low and selling high. The corollary is buying high and selling even higher, but in doing this some of the profit potential is extracted from the trade as a result of the quest for more certainty. Of course the converse is true for opening a short position: sell high, buy low.

This raises the obvious problems—if not occupational hazards—associated with successful speculation. Speculators are often going to be wrong, and speculators are often too early. And how do you handle the winning trades wisely? Again, SuperTraders embrace these features of their job and turn them into positives. If there is a probability of being wrong then it must be acknowledged and dealt with—and this, of course, strengthens the SuperTrader's position as it means he or she is more likely to be on the ball than most others.

For example, a gambler takes a position that buys at $5.00, and then leaves it to chance. A speculator, on the other hand, will have a predefined point at which to recognise that the position is wrong, and that indicates it may lose big-time if nothing is done about it. So the speculator will only be prepared to stake a small amount to confirm the conjecture. If this is, say, 1 per cent, then the speculator enters the position at $5.00 prepared to risk 5¢ for a potential reward of $5.00, if it goes to $10.00. But at $4.95 the position is closed (that is, sold) without procrastination. The gambler, on the other hand, can potentially lose the lot.

A key function of speculation is the preservation of capital in this high-risk business. This means that the speculator is not attached to any one conjecture. It's just a bet. If the conjecture is wrong, the loss is stopped to transfer the risk onto somebody else, and the spectator calmly moves on to the next opportunity

Since the speculator must of necessity operate before the full range of information about the security becomes available, some positions will inevitably be entered too early. What this means is that the speculator's position will be closed at $4.95, and of course the price of the security could then reverse and move rapidly towards $10.00.

What is the speculator's task in this case? Give up? Lament the vagaries of markets? Think back to overtaking that slow car on the road. If you commence your overtaking manoeuvre and a car appears in the opposite direction, you retreat behind the slow vehicle, let the car coming from the opposite direction pass by, and then overtake if it is still possible.

So the speculator's task is to re-enter the position at $5.00. Market re-entry is a powerful tool in the hands of an astute speculator who knows that there is a good chance that the original conjecture was correct, just premature.

On the other hand, what if the security exited at \$4.95 falls sharply? This is to the speculator's advantage too. Instead of buying at \$5.00 the market is providing the opportunity to re-enter at a very much lower price, if its eventual ascent to \$10.00 is still indicated. That is to say, if the original conjecture still holds true.

And of course while waiting patiently for this security to reverse, the SuperTrader is looking for other opportunities to exploit.

While enacting great defence is important if the position is wrong, the crucial element in this business is to effectively process those conjectures that turn out to be right. Handling winners requires its own special mindset. In the car, the goal is to reach your destination safely and as expeditiously as the traffic allows. In trading, the goal is to make consistent profits as safely and expeditiously as the market allows.

A SuperTrader, in a measured and deliberate way, adds to winning positions so that more is at stake in those positions that are proving themselves. How do you know that you are on a winner? Your account is increasing. While there is a temptation to take the profit just because it's available, an increasing account is not a signal to close out (unless the position starts to retrace and hits a defensive stop) but actually to buy more. Remember in the house auction: the vendor did not stop the auction when her \$1 million reserve was met.

Figure 1.4: flexibility—probing for the best entry

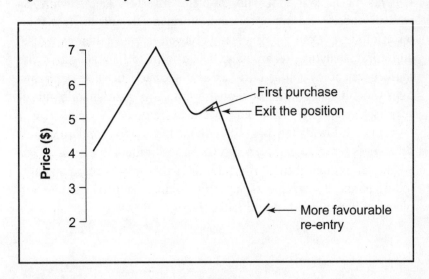

Handling winners is more than passively riding them. The job is to extend and manage the winning position in full cooperation with the rising market. This is the key to super profits. Again, patience is the key: waiting for information to become available to the crowd so that the crowd feels that buying is now quite safe. The speculator is then in a position to provide the crowd with what it wants.

The winning trade will eventually have to be closed in order to book a substantial profit. The profit from successful speculations well and truly covers the cost of fossicking for winning positions, as well as providing a handsome return for effectively managing risks, as the speculator goes about his or her business

Each SuperTrader that I work with applies this approach in a unique way to develop an effective niche or edge in terms of time periods and trading instruments. For some, holding a large position with a 5-point risk on the SPI for five minutes seems like an eternity. Others hold positions in commodity markets like Pork Bellies for months. But they all operate their speculation in a proactive, businesslike and detached manner.

Gamble, invest or trade for profit?

Financial markets can accommodate anyone, with any approach. They are neutral and democratic. If you want to dabble, you can. If gambling is your thing, no problem. Investors are welcome, as well as those who want to commit financial suicide, test their testosterone, live out their personal grievances, prove their expertise, and apply analytical techniques. If you want to be a spectator, the market welcomes you too. In fact as a spectacle markets are better than watching a sporting or drama event. They are dynamic, full of surprises ... and they never end. Markets are potentially addictive.

In the following few pages, I'll define for you the similarities and differences between gamblers, investors and traders.

My definition of the term 'trading' is the process of buying and selling financial instruments *for profit*. In financial markets there are plenty of hopeful and unprofitable 'traders'.

Active versus passive investors

The way I see it, there are two distinct ends of the wealth generation spectrum:

⇢ Taking personal responsibility for trading in markets

⇢ Delegating investment decisions to professional managers.

I would call the first trading, or active investing. The second falls under the heading of passive investing. What separates the two? You'll need to ask yourself the following questions: do you have enough talent for trading to manage at least part of your wealth generation yourself? Do you want your profit management licence?

I am using the terms trader and active investor here in a similar vein. So where you see the term trader used it is understood that the same applies to active investors as well. Although the timeframes and levels of activity may differ, both are engaged in making profits by buying and selling. They both achieve the growth of their wealth through personal effort, skill and active control.

A passive investor will delegate financial responsibility (and the need for skill, knowledge and research) to someone else in order to pursue wealth generation. In our house auction example, a passive investor who buys for $1.35 million doesn't care about the future value of the house: he simply wants to live in it or rent it. Selling it for an immediate profit isn't an issue.

Trading and passive investment in financial markets have a number of attributes in common. Both apply to markets over which the trader or investor has absolutely no control. Returns are dependent on what the market offers. There is nothing that a trader or passive investor can do to make the market move a particular way. For those used to getting their way, this can be disconcerting.

In essence both the trader and the passive investor are speculating about the future. Even someone investing in government bonds is speculating that the spending power of the holding is not diminished by inflation in the future.

Another major similarity is that both rely on the effect of compounding, although the effect of compounding is much more marked the higher the rate of return. A passive investor who receives 8 per cent on $100000 will have $1000000 in approximately 29 years. An active investor or trader achieving 24 per cent on the same amount will have a million in fewer than 10 years. Furthermore, with a 29-year time horizon, a trader achieving 24 per cent will need to start with only $1050 to reach the million-dollar mark in that time.

However, the risk/reward profile of the two approaches is quite different. Remember the relationship: the higher the risk, the higher the return.

Essentially traders are seeking a much higher return with a much smaller outlay. To achieve a superior return the trader identifies and manages high-risk positions. A trader will probably specialise in a few types of issues, say stocks, commodities or currencies. Rather than diversify, most of the eggs are being put in one basket and that basket then managed diligently.

Immediately the high-risk position turns against the trader, the position will be liquidated to prevent losses or to lock in profits. In essence the risk is flicked onto someone else. To achieve high returns on a small amount of capital, the trader may employ the advantages of leverage, that is, using other people's money, being extremely careful not to allow the losses that leverage would magnify.

A passive investor's approach to risk is quite contrary to the trader's. The passive investor trades off risk, generally diversifying to the extent that the risk is greatly lessened. Investors do not put all their eggs in one basket. Consequently the return is lowered. This is a sensible strategy because once a diversified portfolio of cash, domestic and international equities, property, absolute return funds, as well as using different managers, is established then the ongoing management of risk is not an issue for the individual. Over a period of time a fully diversified portfolio shouldn't be very volatile and its returns should be in line with the average—which means, mediocre returns.

There's a metaphor I'm fond of that summarises these differences: a passive investor drifts with market tide, whereas a trader goes places by sailing with the market wind.

Many erroneously believe that trading is merely the application of technical or fundamental analysis, and that buying a computer program that does this can ensure success. This, of course, is unfortunately not the case. Yes: analytical methods are the tool of a trader, but the process of successful trading requires more than just one tool—in fact a whole set of behaviours and skills. These skills aren't harder, just different.

Since a trader must take responsibility for his or her account it goes without saying that a trader will never rely on tips, broker recommendations or 'black box' computer programs to make decisions.

Nonetheless, there is nothing so special about the business of trading to warrant it being considered glamorous or obligatory. There is nothing wrong with delegating your investment decisions to others.

Delegation to reliable and competent professionals is the way to go if you do not wish to take at least some personal control over your income generation and wealth. But remember delegation does not remove speculation and uncertainty for you. You are relying on portfolio diversification and for markets to be efficient in the long run to provide returns that will be around the average. Delegation is expensive too. Suppose to return 10 per cent on your $1 million portfolio, your management fee is 1.5 per cent. This means to earn $85 000 you would have to spend $15 000. So your management fee is 15 per cent of your return. Furthermore, you pay the management fee even in years of negative returns. So a passive investor spends a significant amount of money each year to achieve a mediocre overall return.

Fundamentally, trading is absorbing and rewarding for those with the aptitude and the will to be successful at it. Taking responsibility for a component of one's wealth generation gives a sense of independence and achievement. It saves expensive management fees. Moreover, as I show in chapter 2, trading as a business properly undertaken is very secure; it provides the added advantage of allowing you to retain and, if you choose, to increase wealth in downward moving markets by short selling. (That is, entering the market by selling wih the aim of buying back the position after a decline.)

A trading component can add to the diversification and return of a well-balanced portfolio. You need to seriously consider the role that trading, operated as a business as shown in this book, can play in your goal to generate and maintain your wealth.

Table 1.1 shows a summary of the similarities between trading and passive investing.

Table 1.1: similarities/differences between trading and investing

Similarities	Differences
No control over markets	Risk/reward profile
Speculating about the future	Diversification versus specialisation
Compounding	Management: delegation or personal
	Level of return
	Relative size position

Trader … or gambler?

Now let's turn our attention to comparing trading and gambling. In my experience most who believe they are 'trading' are in essence gambling. And gamblers lose in the long run. Remember what I said earlier: go through too many red lights and you will ultimately crash.

Let's review the example in figure 1.5. A gambler bets that the equity will rise from $5.00 to $10.00. If he is correct then he makes a $5.00 profit. After entering at $5.00, if he retains the view that the stock should be $10.00, and then does nothing while the stock plummets to $4.00, then he has lost 20 per cent. If it crashed to zero he would lose the lot. It's rare, but it can happen. Think of Enron, HIH and OneTel.

The trader, on the other hand, is out of the bet when the price starts its descent, and loses only 5¢, or 1 per cent. So the trader has very good odds. He is trying to convert 5¢ into $5.00, and will do so if he can sell at $10.00. Furthermore, the trader can add to the position as it becomes favourable, put his foot down in driving terms, and gain much more for his correct bet.

Figure 1.5: gambling versus trading

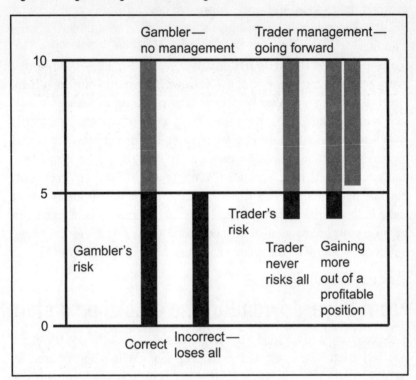

Let me give you another illustration.

At the racecourse the gambler analyses the field and backs what he believes to be the winner. The race starts and there is nothing the gambler can do. If the horse he bet on wins, he collects. If it loses (more likely because there are many horses in the race), he tears up his betting slip.

The trader takes an active approach. She bets on what she thinks is the winner. But it gets left at the starting barrier. She can choose now to relinquish a little of her original bet and then place the remainder on the one she believes is most likely to win now. If she keeps doing this, she must eventually be on the winner.

We can extend example this a little further. An active investor may be interested in the whole race. A very short-term trader may be interested in the winner in the middle 250 metres, while the jobber or intraday trader bets on the winner over the last 20 metres. Who has the best chance of being right on the money?

The big difference between a gambler and a trader is this: A gambler takes risk and then takes whatever result eventuates. A trader takes risk *but then manages it* to achieve a profitable outcome overall.

A profitable trader is like a driver. A driver takes a huge risk every time the car goes out of the driveway. Even on your quiet back street at 60 kph you can be killed. Driving along a freeway at 110 kph is exceedingly dangerous. You are in a plastic and steel projectile with huge momentum and kinetic energy. The driver knows this and manages the car moment by moment so that the risk is controlled and the journey safe. Financial markets are a risky environment, but not nearly as risky as driving a car. Your physical life is not at stake. But nevertheless the risk in financial markets must be managed because your financial life is at stake. Your job as a trader is to manage moment by moment the risks so you can be consistently profitable.

From buyer to vendor: the crucial next step

It seems strange to highlight the fact that you can't make a profit until you sell what you bought, if what you bought has appreciated in price. Nonetheless this is a point that needs to be made. Selling is the key to successful trading. Once you've bought, you need to swiftly stop thinking like a buyer and begin to think like a vendor, because this is what facilitates the profit.

Trading involves the management of risk in a competitive environment. Any current position may quickly turn against the direction of your bet. In fact, in the pursuit of risk, a majority of the trader's initial positions may be wrong. Consequently the trader's job is to quickly exit wrong positions and increase equity in positions that do work out. This sounds easy in theory but most can't do it without experience or training. It requires anticipation, discipline, insight and tenacity.

Did you hear the joke about the woman who heard on the news that a car was driving in the wrong direction down the freeway? Concerned, she phoned her husband to alert him. She said, 'Some idiot is driving down the freeway in the wrong direction.' He replied, 'I know, but there are hundreds of them!'

If you drive the wrong way against the market flow you will lose.

To prevent that happening, think of it this way. Once you have entered a position, transfer your role to that of vendor. By doing this, you have released your attachment to your entry. You've kept in control of your emotions. Now, you'll be able to remain with the flow rather than being blinded by the fact that you've just bought.

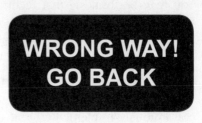

With this clear-eyed view, you're in a position to act. If the price declines then your position is going the wrong way. Don't proceed. Slam the brakes on. Reverse to safety. If prices are increasing, keep going with the position. Profit is accumulating and you are on the way to your destination.

Nevertheless you have to sell at some stage to book the profit. Stepping into the role of vendor changes your perspective in the trade, helps you to lucidly observe the deal flow and places you psychologically in the role of driver; that is, profit manager.

Personal requirements for success

In my work I have witnessed a large number of diverse accounts. You've now read a bit about the SuperTraders I work with and how they go about their business. The important thing to note is that each SuperTrader goes about achieving success differently.

As a coach I have been privileged to work with 'ordinary' people who have changed poor returns into consistent and growing profits. What, then, is the breakthrough for these successful traders?

I've assisted hundreds of clients become successfully profitable at trading, and in doing so, I have noticed four attributes that are shared by all of those clients. The attributes are:

⇢ a personalised approach

⇢ discipline

⇢ passion

⇢ goals.

Let's examine each attribute in turn.

A personalised approach

You may be thinking that technical or fundamental analysis is the key. I have observed traders who use either or both (and, in a few cases, neither) and they all achieve success. The turning point for success is when the trader accepts complete responsibility for the trading account and management of the profits that flow.

The successful trader has developed a unique edge that is continuously implemented and developed. I'll elaborate upon this in chapter 8.

My mantra as a coach is that the business of trading requires the practice of stopping losses and harnessing winners. You must be in control of yourself and your account in all market conditions. Successful traders will do things in their own way, compatible with their own trading style and method. All of them, however, will anticipate these tasks before the market has confirmed them. They are looking forward through the windscreen in anticipation. This signifies personal preparedness and control. These successful traders do not sit back passively being churned around by the market.

Successful traders treat conventional wisdom with circum-spection. Let me give you an example. Most books and courses suggest that a set of details about a particular trade be written down or checked on a list before the trade is ordered. Do you know what? Most of my really successful clients just execute the trade because they *know* their criteria have been met. (Of course they do still systematically record the order and execution details of their trade.) For some a bureaucratic approach is suitable; for others it is an impediment. It just depends on each trader's personal approach.

It's important to note that the market can easily discount an approach that is used by many traders. In other words, if you do the same thing as everybody else, it isn't an edge. This is the problem with programmed black box trading systems. Your personalised approach is durable and successful because it is unique in an ocean of market participants.

Discipline

Discipline is a personal attribute with two facets, one relating to account management and the other to self-management. As in driving a car, you have to do what you have to do to reach your destination.

Successful trading is not a hit or miss affair. Success comes from the will to win and the determination and endurance to follow through. Successful traders take a hard-headed approach and regard their enterprise as a business rather than an indulgence or hobby. They expect their accounts to accumulate, despite being in unproductive trades quite often. They know that with discipline they will prevail.

Successful traders have the discipline to remain focused on their business tasks despite events occurring outside their control such as panic and volatility. They know that success comes from thinking and doing those things that are required of them in any market condition, without negative emotion.

Obviously handling losses requires discipline; but so too does account accrual and ongoing success.

Passion

Another attribute successful traders have in spades is passion. By passion I do not mean an emotional connection to trading. Instead, I mean enthusiasm, motivation and the commitment to stay with the task, especially as pressure comes on, as it inevitably will.

My clients really enjoy their trading. Is this surprising? Success breeds success. Trading isn't an ordeal; rather it's a challenge. The successful traders aren't ambivalent about it: they want to do it profitably, and do it well. Setbacks do not dent their confidence and enthusiasm (for long) but are regarded as an opportunity to learn and refine their methods. Passion enables them to self-evaluate and strive for better outcomes.

Passion emanates from the fact that their trading or investing business satisfies, as well as profits, deep psychological needs. We will review these in the chapter on psychology.

Goals

Setting a direction and benchmarks is extremely important in life—and in the trading business. You have to know where you are going so that you can take responsibility for getting there. I ask clients to set specific yet challenging goals.

I have a goal for you now. Your goal is to work through this book, and prepare yourself seriously to attain your licence to profit. This is an opportunity for you to first learn the processes and skills properly and then apply what you have learnt, laying the foundation for your own wealth creation through trading profitably in financial markets.

Summary

Do you realise that driving your car is an extraordinary thing to do? Your great-great-grandparents would certainly be in awe of your ability to drive a car. They might even see it as supernatural. Yet it seems commonplace to you because you do it so regularly and successfully. You have attained your licence, and you practise the skills every time you drive.

So it's true—ordinary people *can* do extraordinary things. Likewise, you can achieve extraordinary things in financial markets.

In the next chapter we are going to examine how to make your trading safe, and I'll also give you some specifics on how to reach your destination.

Road rules: performance standards

In the previous chapter we established that to become successful in trading in financial markets, you need to be able to handle uncertainty. You need to be able to deal with uncertainty about the future in a way that enables to reach your destination, just like you do when you drive your car.

Another word for uncertainty is risk. In this chapter I will show you the foundation that allows you to manage risk with consistent and predictable success.

Case study: amateur to professional

One client, let's call him Phillip, who approached me several years ago for professional assistance had learned at an analysis-software user group that you should buy every time a short-term moving average moves up to penetrate a longer term moving average that is going sideways or up. This is exactly what Phillip did. He had

$400 000 and made 40 trades worth $10 000. Figure 2.1 shows his profit/loss statement for the financial year.

Figure 2.1: actual record of an amateur account

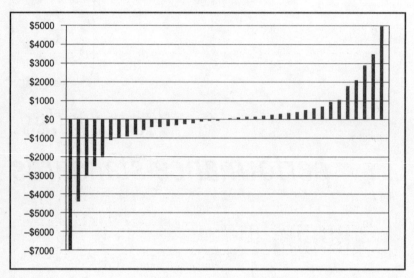

Have a good look at the data in figure 2.1. The worst trade Phillip made was a $7000 loss, and the best a winner of almost $5000. You can see that there were a few big losers and a few good winners. The large losers drained Phillip not only psychologically but also financially. The big losers represented lost opportunity to profit. Over half of his trades sat in the range between a loss of $500 and a profit of $500.

Of course Phillip was frustrated and disappointed because overall, despite his intention to profit, he had lost money. Maybe after reading chapter 1 you'll be able to guess what Phillip's error was. Yes: he wasn't a vendor. He held the positions without selling any of the losers.

Let's examine figure 2.2, which shows the outcome if Phillip had done his job as a trader and sold any position when it lost 10 per cent of the original stake.

You can see the dramatic impact of cutting the losers with a stop loss line at minus $1000. While the vertical axis has been rescaled, the data is exactly the same. You can see that the value of the profitable trades above the line is greater than the losses below the line. By selling out the losers, Phillip now has an edge. Furthermore, he has 'saved' an extra $13 000 or $14 000 to find winners.

Figure 2.2: preventing losses

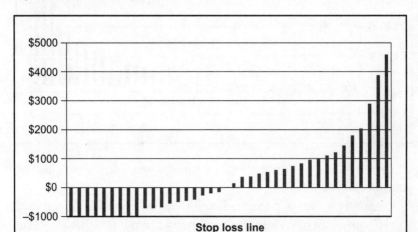

Can we improve this situation?

In figure 2.3 (overleaf) we have placed the stop loss 2 per cent or $200 away from the purchase price of $10 000 for each position. Again I must emphasise that the data is identical to the original. We haven't changed the data but we have managed it. You will note that the tighter management has magnified the edge: profits are much greater than the losses. Not only does proper and consistent active management greatly enhance returns, it is much safer than a hands-off approach. What makes driving the car safe is continuous and active management. You can't take your hands off the wheel.

The stop loss is a protective measure. It's just like using the brakes when you drive your car. Why do cars have brakes? So they can go *faster* and *further*. Can you imagine driving a car that lacked brakes? Of course not! You wouldn't be able to progress safely with any pace whatsoever. Similarly in trading you need to use the stop loss to retain control. The stop loss is your brake pedal.

Figure 2.3: trading is very safe

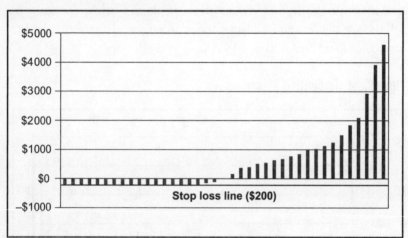

Stop loss line ($200)

Of course when you drive there are times when you are able to put your foot down.

Similarly in businesslike trading it's sensible to make more out of your good winners. When the conditions are right—that is, when your position is winning and looks set to continue to do so, then you can add to your position in order to make the most out of being on a winner. Loading up is how you achieve superior profits.

Figure 2.4 shows the account of a professional trader. It is the same data as Phillip's, but it is handled properly. This series of graphs has identified for you the defensive and attacking processes required to run a consistently profitable trading business.

And what happened to the client whose data we have been reviewing? Today he is a very successful professional trader.

Probability: the foundation of the business

Look again at the first data set in this chapter. When you look at it overall it seems to correspond to a normal probability distribution or a bell curve. Results are distributed between a few large losers to a few large winners while most trades are in the 'ho hum' range of small losers and small winners. It has to be this way because we are dealing with uncertainty. The best way I know to represent uncertainty is to use (or invoke) a normal probability distribution.

Figure 2.4: going for superior returns

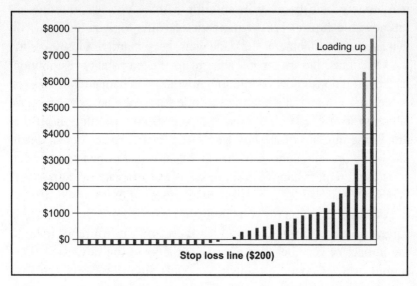

Stop loss line ($200)

Figure 2.5: speculators must act

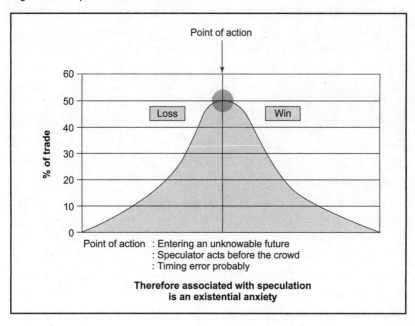

When you enter a trade you don't know the outcome. As illustrated in figure 2.5, when you enter at the point of action there are only two possibilities: the position could either win or lose. There is a real anxiety here because in entering a trade you are entering an unknowable future. It is a moment of truth for you in terms of managing the outcome. If the trade wins, keep it and if it loses, cut it.

Of course, life in general adheres to the probability distribution pattern. You don't know your future. Anything can happen. Most events in life are routine, but sometimes wonderful things can occur such as falling in love, the birth of a baby, or unexpected promotion. At the same time rare but disastrous events can occur: the accidental death of a loved one, a diagnosis of cancer, or dismissal from a secure job.

It is difficult to control the outcome of these negative occurrences. Where it is possible, it is prudent to do so. For example, if you discover a melanoma on your body you would immediately have a surgeon cut it out. You take out life, house and car insurance to limit the impact of very negative events (outliers) in the rare event they should occur. Generally, though, you can't alter these very negative events in your life but instead have to accept them.

The huge advantage in trading (as in driving your vehicle) is that you can, and in fact you *must*, exert management control. This means you can guard against experiencing these negative events, and furthermore manage to pursue and magnify the positive outliers.

So even though the future is uncertain and unknowable in trading, you can manage the outcomes so that you must profit. In markets, properly managed, uncertainty is your friend.

I'm not suggesting that you can change the market: that's not possible. Your task is to identify what the market is doing moment by moment and correspondingly do what you have to do to create and secure your success.

Figure 2.6 shows the normal distribution of trade outcomes. Applying a stop loss is how you can control the uncertainty that exists when you enter a position. The probability distribution indicates that half of your trades will not be successful. But you must accept the unsuccessful trades because if you don't, you do not avail yourself of the opportunity to experience the winners. Another way of saying this is that you must take the risk.

What the stop loss line does is prevent you experiencing the larger negative outliers. The stop loss line is where you predetermine that you will hit the brakes when the trade is initiated.

Figure 2.6: normal distribution of trade outcomes

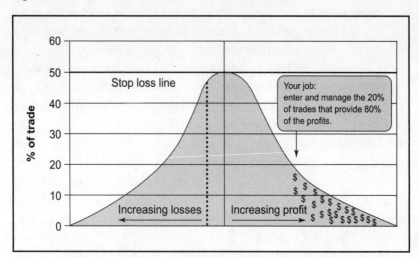

It is important to remember that the money you expend to identify the winners is not a loss overall, because it enables you to achieve the winners, and the amount you win covers all the losses and then some. In figure 2.6 the area between the stop loss line and the centre line is the *rent* you have to pay to run a trading business.

I want you to reframe your thinking on this. Just as every business has overheads, your trading business does too. As in every other business, while retaining your edge, the more overhead you pay the more profit you make. I discovered this many years ago when I resolved to make trading a disciplined business. I noticed the more I got stopped out (that is, exited a trade at a predetermined stop loss level), the more money I made. It seems perverse, but it's the reality.

There is another way to regard your trading rent. When you go on a journey in your car do you regard the petrol you use as a loss? No. Although you might grumble about it, you know it's a requirement to go on your journey and to reach your destination. The more petrol you use, the further you can go.

A few more insights can be gleaned from figure 2.6.

Only relatively few winners are really lucrative. In many other businesses you know when the lucrative periods are, for example, Christmas for retailers. You may know who the lucrative customers are, for example, those who place large orders and those who are good payers. Unfortunately, in trading you don't know when Christmas is or at the outset which trade is going to be the good payer. You have to be ready at any time to appreciate and work the really good positions as they arise.

In business you have to keep control of your overhead for sure, but really successful businesses focus on and cultivate the highly profitable periods and customers. You have to do this in your trading business too. You know you will have losers and overheads. Your focus should be on the profit side of the probability distribution: not on hitting the brakes, but on getting to your destination.

So now I have shown you the basis for your trading business using the probability distribution. This is your *edge*—by cutting losers and retaining the profitable trades, you have a profitable edge. Basically, that edge is a biased coin flip.

Now it's time to pin down that edge.

Simulation of 50 trades: applying an edge to the probability distribution

Figure 2.7 reflects the same probability distribution as figure 2.6, but now symbols represent different outcomes. Negative outliers are black holes, negative trades are −, positive trades are + and positive outliers are ★. Using the neutral language of symbols illustrates how to enhance your control over the processes of your trading business.

Figure 2.7 shows that if you trade forever without a stop loss, then you would break even, minus commission and spread. (Spread is the difference between the bid and offer price in the continuous auction.)

Our goal is to never have deep − (minus) or • trades, but to retain the deep + and ★ trades, as long as they remain this way.

As our trade becomes successful we need to trail the defensive stop loss line forward towards the right (see figure 2.8). Remember when a football team kicks off, it brings the defence up near the play. Likewise, when you drive your car you are ready to apply the brakes at any time as your journey advances.

Figure 2.7: normal distribution of trade outcomes shown in symbols

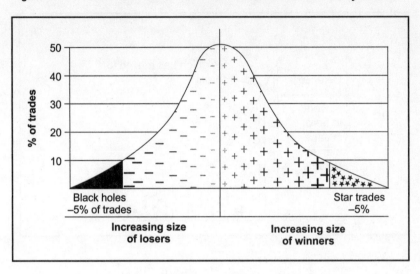

Figure 2.8: putting the probability in your favour

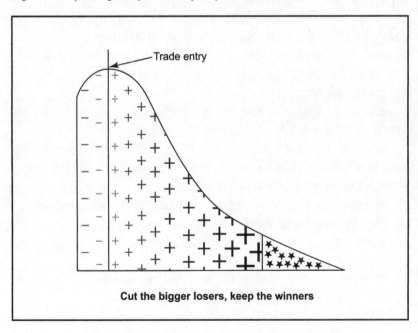

Figure 2.9: defending profitable positions

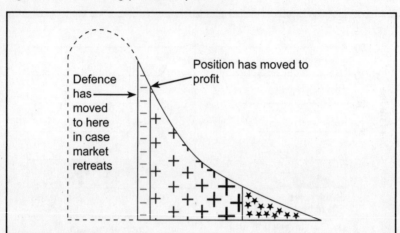

Now it's time to get quantitative in defining our edge.

The major issue that both new and experienced traders have to come to terms with is that it is really a numbers game.

What makes the normal distribution work is a large sample size: enough flips of the coin. Now we are going to equip you with the essence of handling probability as a trader with a simple simulation. This is the best way I know of to focus your attention really well on the trading numbers game.

All the outcomes of trading are represented in the symbols that match different sections of the probability curve.

• represents the negative outlier black holes that can potentially send you broke. Of course we never hold on to these. We flick them away before they can do to any damage.

− represents the remainder of the trades on the left hand side of the distribution. These are the trades that we pay rent on.

+ are the majority on the right hand side of the probability curve, the plus trades.

★ represents the positive outliers that pay us really well: the ★ trades. We want these.

Imagine there are 100 mixed symbols in a bag. To simulate the probability distribution, there are 5 •, 45 −, 45 + and 5 ★ in the bag.

In this simulation, a ★ has +6 units of value on average. A + has an average value of +1.5. On the other hand, a • is worth on average –6 units, and a – has a value of –1.5.

However because of our initial stop loss line we never let a • develop into a major loss (cut losers, remember!).We restrict it as well as a – to a value of –1. We don't want deep – , either.

What are the theoretical outcomes of efficiently managed trading? Using a stop, what hit rate can we expect and what edge ratio will occur?

Hit rate is the number of profitable trades as a percentage of the total trades undertaken in the series.

There are a total of 50 + and ★ in the bag of 100 symbols. Therefore the hit rate you should expect in random trades is 50 per cent.

Edge ratio is the value of all the profit divided by the overhead or rent expended to achieve that profit.

In our example the profit is (45 +) × 1.5 plus (5 ★) × 6. This calculates to be 97.5.

Rent is (45 –) × 1 and (5 •) × 1. This adds up to 50. To calculate our edge ratio, we divide 97.5 by 50. This equals 1.95. So without any analysis and by processing a large number of trades expecting random outcomes, we get an edge of 1.95:1. This means for every $1.00 of rent you pay, you earn $1.95. The profit of the business conducted in this fashion is 95 per cent, that is, your edge provides 95¢ profit for every $1.00 on the money you outlaid. You must agree that it is a very worthwhile business.

Forevermore the minimum performance benchmarks for your trading business are a hit rate of at least 50 per cent and an edge ratio of 2. To attain your trading licence you need to demonstrate that you can perform to these standards.

I am now going to show how it works in practice by simulating 50 trades from our bag of 100 symbols.

I am going to make 50 separate draws from an opaque bag. It is opaque so that I do not bias your sample. If it was a transparent bag I would just draw out the ★ and deep +. Trading reality is not like that. Remember—you cannot tell the future!

To maintain the randomness of the exercise I must replace each symbol that has just been drawn out of the bag after I have recorded the result for that trial. (If you drew out all the ★ you would stop trading because you have used up all the big winners. Conversely if you drew out all the • early on then you would skew your thinking that you don't have much to lose. Real markets don't work like that. There are always • *and* ★ in the bag.)

The task: shake the bag of symbols. Draw one out. Record it with a dot against Trial 1 on the data sheet in table 2.1. Replace the symbol, and shake the container again.

Repeat this procedure until you have completed 50 random and independent trials.

What I have just done is simulate a random sample of 50 trades in sequence.

Now we are in a position to calculate the vital statistics of hit rate and edge ratio, and the amount of profit. As well as this information we will be able to determine:

···→ Number of wins in a row = uninterrupted sequence of + and ★, to identify statistical hot streaks, that is, an uninterrupted sequence of negative outcomes.

···→ Number of losses in a row = uninterrupted sequence of − and •, to identify statistical cold streaks

···→ Number of premium trades = number of ★.

Table 2.1 shows the results of 50 random 'trades' that I conducted for you. I have not doctored this data in any way. Just like in the actual market, you have to take what comes.

I've added up the number of symbols in each column to calculate our trading statistics:

Hit rate = 26/50, 0.52 or 52 per cent
Edge ratio = 36 + 12/24 = 48/24 = 2.00
Profit = 2 − 1/1 = 1 or 100 per cent
Number of wins in a row: 5
Number of losers in a row: 5
Number of premium trades: 2

So our 50 trade series of drawing symbols at random matched the theoretical data.

Table 2.1: results of 50 random trades

Trial	●	–	+	★
1		✓		
2				✓
3			✓	
4				✓
5			✓	
6		✓		
7			✓	
8		✓		
9		✓		
10		✓		
11			✓	
12		✓		
13			✓	
14		✓		
15		✓		
16		✓		
17			✓	
18			✓	
19		✓		
20		✓		
21			✓	
22			✓	
23			✓	
24		✓		
25		✓		
26		✓		

Table 2.1 *(cont'd)*: results of 50 random trades

Trial	●	—	+	★
27			✓	
28			✓	
29			✓	
30			✓	
31			✓	
32		✓		
33			✓	
34			✓	
35			✓	
36			✓	
37			✓	
38		✓		
39		✓		
40		✓		
41		✓		
42	✓			
43			✓	
44		✓		
45			✓	
46		✓		
47			✓	
48		✓		
49			✓	
50		✓		
Total of 50	**1**	**23**	**24**	**2**
Impact	**–1**	**–23**	**+36**	**+12**

I have conducted this trading simulation hundreds of times with individuals and in workshops. I never know the outcome of any individual trial. The average of all these trials is 50 per cent and 2. However the hit rate on individual trials has ranged between 40 and 60 per cent. The edge ratio has ranged from 1.5 to 3.

You can see how the edge ratio is sensitive to the ★. If we had achieved zero ★ and instead replaced them with one − and one + then the hit rate would have been 50 per cent and the edge ratio would have reduced to 37/25 or 1.48. Still a satisfactory 48 per cent profit, but it shows the ★, the premium trades, are the cream of our business. I will deal further with the implications of this in chapter 3.

Remember, you cannot afford to cut your winners.

If you flip a coin and come up with heads 10 times in sequence, what is the probability that the next flip is heads? It's still 50 per cent. This is the case in trading too. The outcome of the next trade is independent of the previous trade, unless your psychology is making your selections non-random. This is why the number of wins and losses in a row are important. It's likely to happen in your real trading business. Do you give up if you have five losses in a row? No. Do you get cocky and over-confident when you have five wins in a row? No. You just keep drawing symbols out of the bag, keeping your rent even with each draw and efficiently managing the outcome as it arises.

All you have to do is appreciate the meaning of each different symbol and act upon it.

To reflect the real trading situation, each time you initially draw a symbol out of the bag you won't be able to see which one you've drawn. It has the grey of the unknown. Only in the future does it become apparent. And of course the symbols aren't fixed; as the trading situation changes, what looks like a winning trade can turn back into a loser. Ideally we want our draw (or trade) to change from unknown to − to ★. But equally it could change to + then back to −, or once underway for some time, from ★ through + to −.

We can't hold a − in the hope that it will change into a + because it could become the disastrous •. (Remember, if you have a melanoma you cut it out, you just don't watch it getting worse. If your meat goes off and becomes rotten in your refrigerator, do you keep it in the hope that it will improve? No, you toss it out and replace it.)

This is why trading management skills are so important: to take advantage of the winning trades, and to protect against negative movement in the market.

Because the market is always changing we have to be alert, and in fact anticipate change, and control our position as the change occurs. This is why trade management is imperative.

Here is the list of moves that we want to happen and to nurture:

⇢ unknown to + (frequent)

⇢ + to ★ (infrequent)

⇢ unknown to ★ (very infrequent).

This is when we are ready to employ attack management skills, to put our foot down. Following is the list of moves that we have to defend against:

⇢ unknown to − (frequent)

⇢ + to − (frequent)

⇢ ★ to − (frequent)

⇢ unknown to • (very infrequent).

If these events occur we employ defensive management skills. We hit the brakes. We just don't want a + to become a −. Similarly we have to be prepared to have a − that we've cut become a + and act accordingly. That requires a re-entry of the position.

The exercise suggests another management issue. Knowing that when you enter the trade it is going to be unknown initially, and that half your trades are going to be negative, implies that your entry position size should be small and you should increase your position size only if it progresses from unknown to + to strongly + to ★.

I am a proponent of having a large number of small initial bets, flicking the losers and working the winners.

Benchmarks for profit

Below is a summary of what we have learned from this example.

⇢ hit rate: profitable trades as a percentage of the total

⇢ edge ratio: return for the amount risked

⇢ profit rate: return minus risk as a percentage of risk

⇢ number of wins in a row

⇢ number of losses in a row

⇢ frequency of superior trades.

The hit rate that you need to aim for is at least 50 per cent and the edge ratio is at least 2:1. If you're not achieving these benchmarks, then you are doing something to sub-optimise your results. (Note that these are minimum benchmarks, enough to gain your trading licence. I have clients who achieve a hit rate of 70 per cent and an edge ratio of around 6. I will explain how to get to this level in the final chapter.)

These figures mean that the profit on your rent (rather than your total capital) is 100 per cent. Why is it so important to know these figures?

Every professional and businessperson has to compare performance with a benchmark. A golfer, for instance, compares his or her score to par. Knowing your figures allows you to budget and plan your profits and income. Every sustainable business has a performance budget: it has to know its edge and then franchise its operations.

In figure 2.10 (overleaf). I have sorted out the ● with − (the rent) and the + and the ★ trades (the return) into two separate piles. You will note the number of symbols in each pile is the same (hit rate 50 per cent) but the money associated with the + and the ★ trades combined is twice that of the other pile (edge ratio 2:1)

Furthermore, as you keep trading, the profit grows.

So if you want to book a $100 000 profit in a financial year, then the rent will be $100 000 while the + and ★ amount will be $200 000. This means you would have to take 200 trades at $1000 risk, or 400 trades at $500, or 800 trades at $250 risk. Of course this formula works pro rata for the level of profit you desire: for example, for a $1 million profit, just multiply the dollar amount of these figures by 10.

Figure 2.10: dollar value versus number

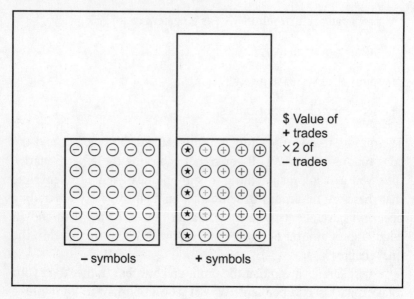

- symbols   + symbols

You will notice that these benchmarks work with even amounts of initial risk. Keeping your bets even in a tranche of 50 trades is important. Suppose your level of risk per trade is $500 and you suddenly go with a $5000 risk. Can you see this last trade has 10 times the risk and the outcome of this trade will distort the benchmark figures?

Knowing your benchmarks will allow you to nominate the reward you want for the time period as well as the amount of activity required to meet the target. You now have a business franchise that you can ratchet up as your competence and experience builds.

The number of wins in a row is important too. You will experience a statistical hot streak in your trading outcomes. When you drive you can get a bunch of green lights in a row. It's not because you have developed a special omnipotence as a driver. The lights don't go green just for you. They would be green whether you were there or not. The next light could be red. If so, you must heed it.

Hot trading streaks are preferable and pleasurable. But this does not mean that you have overcome the randomness and independence of each separate trade. It's just that the numbers can work out this way. You cannot lose concentration or take your hands off the wheel, because the hot streak will end. You need to be ready for that at all times.

The fact that trading is a probability numbers game means that you will have cold streaks too. But this doesn't necessarily reflect your trading ability, just as having a series of red lights doesn't mean you're a bad driver. It just happens.

Knowing that a bad run can happen is a significant insight into how you ought to plan your business. This is why I advocate prudence with entry risk. You should begin trading with only a small amount of your trading capital so that the impact of drawdowns of your capital (that is, capital lost) is not debilitating.

In your trading life you should plan to account for a cold streak that has 20 losers in a row. I hope this won't happen, but there is a possibility (in fact, the probability is 0.5 to the power of 20). However, I have seen professional trading accounts that have had this experience. Is it possible to have 20 red lights in a row?

This worst case scenario should impact on your decisions about the level of risk per trade at entry so that your account should quickly recover if the cold streak is ever experienced.

Figure 2.11 shows the impact on a trading account with entry risk set at different percentages.

Figure 2.11: entry risk management

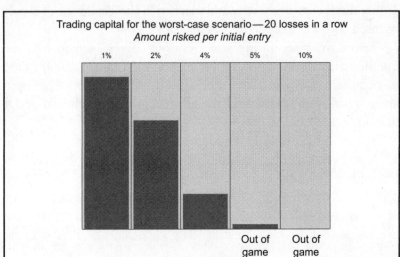

If you bet 5 per cent or more in each trade at entry and experience the worst case scenario, then you are broke, crashed, blown out of the game, no money left. It's over. Another road fatality statistic!

Even at 2 per cent of capital with the worst case scenario you have lost 40 per cent of your capital. It's much easier to come back from a drawdown of 20 per cent which results from a 1 per cent entry per trade.

This is further support for having a large number of small risk trades at entry. Tossing money at a market won't make you win. In fact it's dangerous driving. Small initial bets and following up by going bigger on the winners is the logical and practical way to go.

I don't want to dwell on losers and worst case scenarios however. We want to be positive; to focus on and secure success. This is why we have to know the quantity and the quality of our superior trades.

In the calculations of the benchmarks in the simulation example, I averaged a ★ at +6 units of risk. We saw that ★, although rare—arising only 5 per cent of the time in the probability distribution—really help our edge ratio. Some ★ have a much higher return than +6. An occasional ★ can be +20.

You have to be ready for the positive outliers even though they are abnormal. Because they are rare they act out of the ordinary; they seem different. Needless to say a ★ seems to go whoosh and defy expectations. However they can contract as quickly as they expand. To handle the ★ with skill and alacrity is the challenge of newly licensed and very experienced traders alike.

Before we move on from the discussion about benchmarks, the question arises: which is the most significant? I think the edge ratio is, because it tells you about the edge of your business. It tells you about your overall profit and the efficiency with which you derive that profit.

Hit rate isn't really as important. If you put your money into 10-year government bonds you will achieve a hit rate of 100 per cent but with a tiny edge ratio. With a good edge you can make good profits with a hit rate of 35 per cent, and you can lose with a hit rate of 90 per cent. In fact a high hit rate can lull a trader into a false sense of prowess that can make one neglect good defence. A sloppy 'Look,

Mum, no hands' mentality can result. One black hole can wipe out an account with a 90 per cent hit rate. I've seen it happen.

What our benchmark discussion tells us is that you can be rich without being right most of the time.

To summarise, the five key functions of a successful trader are:

1 enter

2 stop loss

3 take your next trade

4 work your winners

5 establish and extend your basic business franchise.

Your success is important for you and society

Your task as a trader is to identify, enter and manage positions which seem to be risky. If the market unfolds your way, when appropriate you then distribute (that is, sell) your position to others who were unable to anticipate the market as well as you did.

Actually, as a speculator you are playing a very important role for capitalist society: you help markets function in a coherent way. You contribute to market stability by assuming risk when the majority isn't prepared to. Remember, in capitalism everybody gets paid according to their capacity to manage risk. By being successful you are contributing to the prosperity and freedom of all in a capitalist society.

You are adhering to the adage: 'The greater the risk, the greater the reward'. If you do your job well, you will be rewarded handsomely. It seems simple, doesn't it? But it is hard to do consistently.

When you enter the trade you are entering uncertainty: you are taking a risk. You are betting on the future. Only the future can determine your next action. So when you enter you have to have a predetermined plan for your next move as the future unfolds. You let the market tell you whether to attack or defend.

It's taking the risk that allows you to profit so when you think the probability for success is adequate you have no choice: you must enter the trade.

Entering the trade is like leaving the grandstand and joining the game. Your role is going from spectator to actor. You will get tackled, but you will kick goals as well.

The stop loss is your protection in a financial as well as a psychological sense.

Since you are looking as a trader for high-risk yet high-profit positions, you don't know whether this particular bet will work out. In fact in terms of probability there is only a 50 per cent chance of success, irrespective of your assessment of the fundamental or technical picture. So if your speculation does not quickly materialise, the stop loss allows you to flick the risk onto someone else.

Another reason to stop loss is that a market has the potential to blow you away. You don't want to be in a market operating against you, especially since a negative outlier is a real possibility.

Even if you are in a successful trade it is essential to premeditate and trail stop loss to protect your profits. In other words, you need to follow up your profits with a defensive strategy. You don't want a good profit turning into a loser.

Not taking a loss at the predetermined time or position causes two problems: the account unnecessarily diminishes and the trader is wrecked by the experience. In other words there is a financial and psychological opportunity cost.

Don't become attached to your analysis, your entry or position. Don't identify with this particular trade. You will possibly have hundreds or thousands of trades in your lifetime. Any one entry isn't all that important. Remember the person on the opposite side of your trade could well be right. Don't resist the market.

Your money management principles mean that your initial trade is only a fraction of your full commitment. The money being stopped out as rent for your right to trade this market is a business cost. Having your stop executed does not indicate a bad trade; it's part of your business expenditure. Ignoring an initial or trailing stop is a loss, an absolute no–no, though. Don't do it.

Been stopped out? Good. Let it go and move forward. Go ahead and look for your next opportunity. Just because you had to stop at a red light, doesn't mean that you should give up on the journey.

When you have been stopped out you need to take the very next trade that your system identifies. Why? Because you don't know which trade is going to be the one that is the real winner for you. The next opportunity might be a ★ trade. You cannot afford to ignore it.

Not taking your next trade causes deep disappointment if it does turn out to be the winner you were seeking. Your next signal may come soon after you have been stopped out. You must take the trade even if the trade is in the same direction and the same instrument as before you were stopped out. This is hard to do, especially if the market speeds away from your initial entry point. Rational analysis will tell you that you were right about the overall direction but a little early with your initial trade. Remember, as we saw in chapter 1, the occupational hazard of a speculator is being too early.

As an experienced trader you have to be alert for stop and reverse opportunities.

Most trading books correctly encourage you to ride your winners. I go a step further: you have to *work* your winners. You have paid your rent. Now is the time to collect, to put your foot down.

The direction and momentum of the market is currently in favour of your trade. The temptation is to close out soon with a profit, to release yourself from the psychological tension of allowing your profits to grow, and to secure a good win at last. Don't succumb to the temptation to complete the trade when it begins to win. Yes, close it out if it actually retreats. However don't exit it because you think it might retreat. It might just be a strong + or ★ trade It has certainly satisfied the criteria for a good outcome. It's winning!

I have worked with clients who were able to follow their signals and stop loss, but failed to carry through on their winning trades to make their overall returns worthwhile. Working winners is what makes the profits grow.

Rather than close out the winner, it is your business to increase your bet in a staggered way so that the position becomes more profitable, as long as the market momentum continues in your favour. This is usually called 'scaling in' or 'pyramiding'. I call it 'loading up'. This is where your big profits are made. Your initial bet is correct, and now you are making it pay off. It will cover all the small previously stopped out positions, and then much more.

Of course your loading up technique has been predetermined with a staking plan. I will present several alternative strategies for this in chapter 5. As your position increases, a suitable trailing stop loss point is determined and enacted if the momentum turns against your position. This protects your accumulated profits.

Part of the plan will be to determine at what point you scale out of your position. Remember it's your business as a trader to distribute the asset you are warehousing for others who could not see the opportunity when you did, or who were not prepared to take the risk as you were.

Once you have the essentials of trading and an edge of 2:1 you have proven your reliability. You have your licence to trade. You now have a basic business franchise which you can expand.

While maintaining your reliability you can go ahead to make this a really worthwhile and lucrative business. This formula applies:

Profit = reliability × size × opportunity

Going forward, after you have attained your trading licence you can increase your profits by taking larger positions and/or trading more positions and markets. Put simply, you can bet bigger and more often if you choose to.

I'll show you more about this in the final chapter of the book. But at the moment I have to remind you that reliability is a function of your hit rate, edge ratio and your psychology squared. That's why it's important to delve into trading psychology (see chapters 4 and 5).

Where amateurs flounder

In this chapter I have laid out in some depth out the essentials for profitable trading. It's basically a numbers game in which, through appropriate management, it is possible to create and sustain a safe profitable edge. An edge in the trading business is similar to what any successful business achieves. In essence, trading is a business just like any other.

The reasons most fail are manifold. Look back to figure 2.1, which charted the performance of an amateur account.

Amateurs do not approach the task in a systematic or businesslike way. Entries are spasmodic rather than systematic, losses aren't stopped and winners are cut short.

The whole focus of amateurs is on entries. The amateur will remain a spectator until it seems safe to enter the market and then hold the position rigidly irrespective of the information the market tells them about how their position is faring. In a sense their strategy is to enter a 'trade' and hope for the best, rather than manage it. In chapter 1 we called this gambling.

An amateur will rationalise that if this trade doesn't work out then it can be put in the bottom drawer as an investment. I'm sure you have heard the old yet cynical joke: 'What's the definition of an investor? A failed speculator.'

Amateurs give up too easily after a few losers. However a worse situation for amateurs is to greatly build up their bet size after a couple of wins. When the inevitable cold streak comes they are vulnerable to being wiped out. When this happens there is a tendency to rationalise their poor management by claiming the market is rigged!

Amateurs do not respect leverage of trading CFDs (contracts for difference), futures, commodity, currency or margin lending accounts. Although leverage magnifies profits, it is magnified losses that amateurs seem to accomplish.

The next level of development is what I call the break-even rut. Here the 'trader' stops losses but doesn't work the winners. Nothing much is lost, but neither is much gained. Here is the scenario. The 'trader' has lost $5000 in five consecutive trades. He does enter the next trade and it is a star one. It whooshes up quickly to $5000. To gain psychological relief he closes out the trade to cover his previous losses and then wonders why he is in the break-even rut. His job was to treat each trade as an independent event—ideally, the last trade should have been worked to its entirety.

What amateurs do is completely underestimate the necessary activity, as well as the cognitive and psychological demands of the business.

Summary

In the chapters so far I have exposed the cognitive demand needed to establish a profitable trading enterprise—the basis of the road rules. You know the cognitive demands of driving a car successfully, and now that you know the cognitive demand for success in trading, it's time to progress your learning.

With the probability approach, I'm not suggesting that you just throw a dart at the board and select trades arbitrarily. Strategy is important. In the next chapter we will examine where you might locate high probability trades. It's time to turn our attention to the road map to help plan the journey to our destination.

Road maps:
optimising analysis

Most books on trading focus on the application of analysis, especially technical analysis, as the answer to trading success. You will notice that this book has only one fairly brief chapter on the subject. Really, analysis is not the critical factor in market success. Analysis is like a road map. It can guide your journey, especially if you are venturing somewhere foreign. It starts you off in the right direction, but it will not get you to your destination. Once you know your route you have to put the road map back into the glovebox and actually drive the car towards your destination.

When you analyse a market with a view to trading it, what are you actually looking for? You are trying to locate the positive and star trades, trying to skew the probability distribution towards high-probability entries to improve your edge.

What you are trying to do is to anticipate or identify price movement that you think might be likely to surge for a sustained period of time. You are searching for those trades that have the highest profit potential. This implies that you are searching for positions that have a high level of risk. You are looking for the beginning of moves and are attempting to detect when the move is nearing its end.

Why reliance on analysis alone can't succeed

There are plenty of analysis methods to employ. Besides technical analysis, which in the computer age has wide usage, there are interest rate levels, pattern recognition, market depth, GDP forecasts, P/E ratios, the impact of news events, dividend yields, not to mention crystal balls, the comparative price of hamburgers between countries, crop reports and astrological events. And so on ad infinitum.

Over the long run, if applied with trading skill and sound money management that we reviewed in chapter 2, analysis can be conducive to, but will not guarantee, a successful outcome. Why? Because when the analysis is wrong the trade will be stopped and when it does pick a winning position it will be worked to the hilt.

It's technical analysis which has the most charm for a newcomer. Technical analysis is the overlay of algorithms, tools and techniques to assist you in perceiving the market. It extrapolates from what's gone on in the past to give you possible scenarios and insights into the future.

Computer-assisted technical analysis is rapid and powerful. You can scan and compare many markets and issues, revealing reversals, break-outs and new trends. It can help you to decide potential targets both in terms of price and time. It can assist you with the placement of initial and trailing stops, and loading up points.

This sounds great—so what is wrong with it? Unfortunately, technical analysis can only ever be conditional. Despite analysis, the market, the sum total of millions of different decisions, will do what it wants to do. It will always surprise. No person, no analysis methods, technical or otherwise, can ever consistently and completely discern the market and what it is likely to do. Remember, the future is unknowable. Even with the best technical analysis, it's the action of the market itself (and therefore the unpredictable actions of the buys and sells and trades that go into making up the market) that determines what you must do. Trusting the market's action is better than trusting an analytical picture of it.

Another problem relates to the objectivity of analysis. In my work I have noticed a tendency for some traders to focus on signals that confirm their general market prejudices. That is, if they are bullish they look for bullish indications and blot out contrary information that their analysis may be presenting. Your analysis is necessarily subjective because you establish the parameters which you think are significant. Just as statistics can always be 'massaged' to tell any story a politician wants them to, using a computer software analysis package does not ensure objectivity.

Technical analysis is available to anyone who can buy a suitable computer program. Don't forget that on the other side of your trade is someone who is holds the opposite view to you. Is it possible that both sides of a trade employ technical analysis? Yes, if they are using different indicators or similar indicators with a different time frame.

But do you realise the counterparty to your trade may be using exactly the same analysis as you? Some astute traders will be scanning the analysis signals of the punters with the deliberate intention of 'fading' them: that is, they will sell when they know that the popular indicators are making the trade seem an obvious buy. Of course this astute trader will stop and reverse if the initial position turns out to be in the wrong direction. (Why not try this yourself under the conditions of the trading gymnasium, which are outlined in chapter 6?)

Another problem with overemphasis on technical analysis is the trader who lets money management principles be overturned by what looks like 'an absolute set-up'. I have dealt with clients who, because of a belief in the infallibility of their analysis, have put their whole stake on the initial position. They have been disappointed when the 'set-up' didn't work out.

Although useful in some ways, no analysis method can guarantee a successful outcome in trading. It's the truth of this statement which causes many analysts never to trade. Analysis is interesting and absorbing but most suitable for spectators and passengers.

Best not have the beautiful analysis sullied by the treachery and unpredictability of the market!

Analysis and trading are two separate functions. Expert analysis doesn't pay. Expert trading does.

Analysis assists with navigation; it cannot tell you where the bends in the road will be, where the road works are, where the slow vehicles are, where the gridlock will be, and whether the traffic lights will be green or red. All these variables have to be discerned and negotiated by the driver as they occur.

Furthermore, it's dangerous for the driver to be gawking at the road map while he is driving. It's a distraction from safe driving.

But the fundamental limitation of analysis is that neither it nor anything else can predict the future. This is the big difference between a road map for a journey and trading analysis. The market 'map' can and will change from moment to moment, while the points on the road-map will never change.

Why does the market map change?

If you have been playing poker with your buddies for a while and you win on every occasion, do you think your buddies are going to let this situation continue? Of course not, if they're at all competitive. You're taking their money! What they will do is find out what makes you win and either do the same as you (and thus reduce your edge) or change what they do so they win and you lose. And so it goes on.

Markets are like this. Their competitive nature will ensure that they change over time. This is exacerbated by the fact that markets have new players entering and departing continually. Yes markets go up, down and sideways but in continually different modes.

Is it any wonder that analysis is unable to predict the future?

When you examine charts of markets in retrospect they always seem logical, reasonable and predictable. They are indeed a collection of fixed points that are unchangeable, just like a road map. This is just one problem with this: as we all know, hindsight allows 20/20 vision.

The problem is, and it is an immense one, that the price of the instrument is being decided now by only a few participants who are determining the shape of the road map by their actions of price discovery now. The price being created by competing buyers and sellers in the moment of time now may be inconsistent with the chart. But when you look at it in retrospect it will seem logical and predictable, even if it did not seem like that at the time.

The market road map is a work in progress, created and recreated every minute of the day by players who are trying to get the best deal for themselves by outsmarting their counterparty.

Predictive methods are fraught with danger. This is because they are attempting to do the impossible—nobody knows the future, and the market doesn't have to conform to any particular prediction. Whatever analytical methods you employ, they will, at best, only provide a speculation, bet, conjecture, guess, hypothesis, estimate, presumption, and/or a premise about the future. The market will either confirm or reject the speculation at some point in the future.

There is another issue with using analysis for prediction, this time a psychological one. Sometimes the person who makes the prediction wants it to be right, regardless of information the market is providing moment by moment. In other words the person becomes so attached to the prediction, so much of their self-esteem and ego is bound up in being right, that they may enter a state of denial if the market moves against the prediction. In effect they are saying the market must be wrong, not their view. These people find it very difficult to close out a loser because that would mean first acknowledging the reality of the situation.

Predictions foster a closed mind, defensiveness, and rigidity—not desirable attributes for trading, or for driving a car. You must be open to the flow as new information comes along. As I said earlier, a successful trader needs to be constantly alert, open to movement and change.

Attempting to make uncertainty certain

I think analysis is sold to newcomers with the delusion that certainty is desirable and possible in markets. There seems to be a hidden agenda here, an encouragement to use analysis to find a 'sure thing' that is as secure as 10-year government bonds but with much higher rate of return. Of course it's in the vested interest of software vendors to encourage this delusion, but nonetheless, people certainly do use analysis to shield themselves from the uncertainty that characterises trading.

My belief is that analysing the risk out of trading ensures poor results. Remember the risk-return relationship. Hours are spent by analysts in the vain hope of finding the elusive certainty in the market, even to the point of analysis paralysis. The temptation is to create confirmation after confirmation, to have all the analytical 'ducks' line up, before the trade is entered. Alas, it is usually too late. Even if it's not too late, much of the profit potential has been exhausted.

Remember the car-overtaking analogy I presented in chapter 1. You need to overtake the slow vehicle at the first clear opportunity. Waiting until the next corner to see what is coming towards you will lead to missed opportunity and frustration. This explains in some degree why people fail at trading. Similarly, they experience missed opportunity and frustration in their trading endeavours.

The situations I have been describing are just the opposite of what is required to make good profits in the market. The goal is to find trades that have a high probability of profit—trades that are very uncertain—and use your driving skills to make the project safe and profitable.

By all means analyse the past if you enjoy doing that. But to create and sustain profits you must trade in the professional and businesslike way described in chapter 2, despite the uncertainty of the present moment, not to mention the future.

Where are the high-probability, high-profit trades?

So is there a role for analysis in profitable trading? My answer is yes. Analysis can help navigate you towards the highly profitable trades. Its role is to identify risk worth taking. Then it's over to the management of the risk in each trade to secure the profit, if it's there.

How are we going to identify risk worth taking?

Put yourself behind that slow vehicle again, wanting to overtake it. Can you pass just because you want to or believe that the road is yours? No, you must watch the traffic for the opportunity. What happens if you overtake into the flow of oncoming traffic? Yes that's right, you crash. You need to wait until you have a clear straight road without any traffic coming towards you. When is the best place to pass: the beginning of the straight, the middle of the straight or the corner? The answer is obvious, isn't it? Overtake at the first available opportunity, just after the beginning of the straight.

This is the best time in terms of taking the risk because the probability of successful overtaking is highest here. This is what we want to do in trading. Take the first available opportunity when the flow isn't against us.

There are two points worth making here. First, as an experienced driver, you don't have to distract yourself by measuring the overtaking distance or your momentum and kinetic energy, relative to the vehicle you are overtaking. You just pass, because you do all these things automatically based on your knowledge of the process. Likewise, in the market you simply enter the trade.

The second point is more significant. In the market setting the 'straight road' is virtual; it doesn't exist yet. Your *assumption* is that the 'straight' is long enough to profit. Only the future can reveal whether this is the case. You have to be very flexible in case it's not so. Nevertheless this should not daunt you. You must take the opportunity when it first presents itself. This is the uncertainty that ensures you profit handsomely overall. This is the uncertainty that the majority avoid.

This is the uncertainty that provides you with your edge.

To illustrate the overtaking analogy in the market setting, let's re-examine the house auction information from chapter 1. See figures 3.1a and 3.2a (overleaf).

When is the best time to buy in this market? It's when the auction starts. When is the best time to sell? When there are no more bids. Did the person who bid at $925000 know that there would be a bid at $950000? No. But that—the uncertainty of trading—is exactly what is required for the vendor to profit.

Figure 3.1a: best time to enter or exit the auction

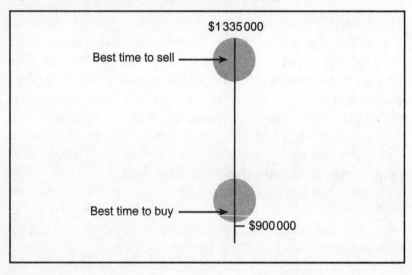

Figure 3.1b: what to do when the auction peters out

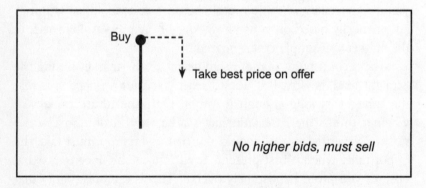

On the other hand, for the person who buys at $925 000 to profit, she has to rely on another bidder doing something she wasn't prepared to do at that time, which is to bid above $925 000. Moreover, did the buyer at $925 000 know the market would zoom up to $1.35 million? No. But by buying at this lower price she knows the probability of a price escalation (that is, the probability of profit), is higher than it would be had she bought at $1.1 million or $1.25 million.

So with this purchase, she is speculating that prices will go higher so that she will make a profit. The amount of information available to make this decision is minimal. As more information becomes available that this is a strong up move, the amount of profit to be made contracts and the risk of entering the position increases.

To the uninitiated this seems counterintuitive. Let's put it in another way. It seems safer to buy at $1.25 million because there is a history of price increase. But it is actually much less safe to buy at $1.25 million than at $925000. Furthermore, the profit potential of buying at $1.25 million is much less than buying at $925000. The goal of trading is not safety, but profit.

Figure 3.2: the inverse relationship between information, profit potential and real risk

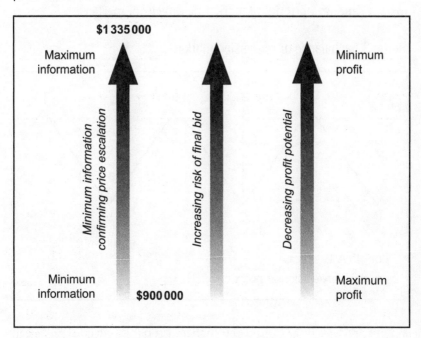

There are a couple more points to be made about the auction market. The analytical task for the bidder at $925000 is to look at what happens immediately after her bid. If she bids at $925000 and there are no higher bids she has to pay up. If there is a higher bid then she still needs to be vigilant in watching the auction as it progresses, to keep reading the market. The up auction could end at any time and consequently she has to sell out to bank her profit.

After her purchase at \$925000 she doesn't know the future. The information upon which she will execute her management actions is yet to emerge. However, that doesn't matter: as long as she competently and confidently manages her position as the future unfolds, she should be able to book her profit.

Unlike the discrete house auction market, financial markets are more or less continuous. They are always moving up, down or sideways. While this adds complexity, the information, profit potential and real risk relationship still applies.

The role of analysis is to reveal the high profit probability trades that harness the complexity rather than being overcome by it.

Figures 3.3a and 3.3b compare a sideways market (a 'regression' market) and an uptrending market (a 'direction' market).

Figure 3.3a: balance or regression market

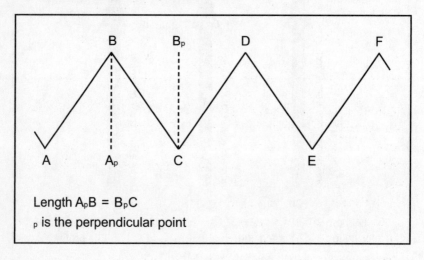

Length $A_pB = B_pC$

$_p$ is the perpendicular point

Where are we going to find the highest probability trade? How can we rate the profit probability to increase our chance of strong profit overall?

Figure 3.3b: up direction market—buy

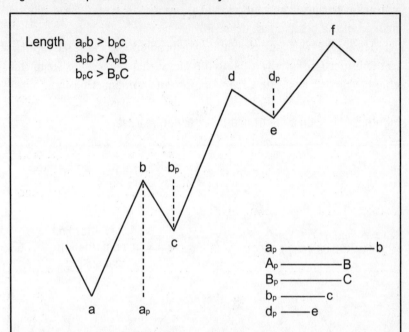

Figures 3.3a and 3.3b show a perpendicular line from the apex point to a horizontal line extended right from the point of origin of that move. The length of the perpendicular line is the profit potential of the trade. As with the house auction example, we want to buy at the base of the line and sell at the top of the line.

In the regression market the length $A_pB = B_pC$.

In the up direction market the length a_pb is much greater than A_pB. After all, this is what defines an uptrend. Conversely, in a down direction market (not illustrated) B_pC is much greater than b_pc.

The length of the lines shows the best probability trade. In figure 3.3b the retracement b_pc is quite steep while d_pe is a shallow retracement.

By far the best trade is to buy just after point a, c or e.

Conversely picking the top in an uptrend is a low probability event. Some erroneously believe the most money is to be made by picking the top of an uptrend. This is like standing in the pathway of a freight train. There will finally be a top but the higher probability sale is just after the first lower peak after the trend has changed. If you want to short the market, sell the peaks in a regression market instead of the peaks in an uptrend.

The logic of this is unassailable. The problem is that it is susceptible to the criticism of analysis using hindsight that I raised earlier in this chapter. So let's examine a realistic present-moment situation.

Figure 3.4: buying a confirmed up direction market

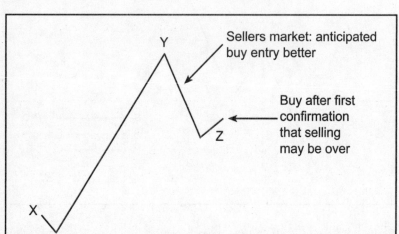

Because it's an uptrend we are looking to enter a high probability position by buying. We are not going to enter a short sale after point Y.

When do you buy? As the market is declining from Y, we sit on our hands. The market is dropping and prices are improving in terms of our eventual purchase. The public are not looking to buy; they are frightened by going against the trend ('retracement'). Remember they bought near the top at Y because they needed so much information before they could act. They are regretful, feel betrayed and might be unloading. However when the selling ceases a reversal will occur. We now have a fixed point Z, and it is the time to buy.

To repeat: you don't buy just because the market is declining. There needs to be some evidence of rally from the down move. When you have the first piece of evidence you can buy to test the market. Waiting for more confirmation just diminishes the profit potential (see figure 3.5).

Figure 3.5: delaying for more confirmation is counterproductive to trading for profit

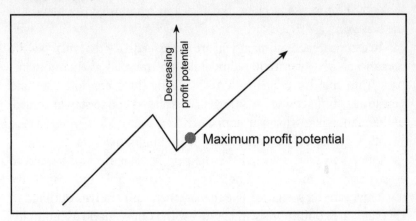

This is similar to buying at $925 000 in the house auction example.

If the market drops below point Z then you sell out for a small loss. If the uptrend is indeed underway you can now load up on your initial trade to test the market.

Now you are using analysis proactively. The road map has allowed you to orient your journey to enter the market at a desirable point. Nevertheless you are always looking at the traffic through the windscreen to determine your next action.

Are there other ways to identify entries for the positive and star trades? Certainly. Nevertheless, using the strategy outlined above, you are now reading the market and planning your trade scenario accordingly. You need to be able to do this to attain your licence to trade.

Scenario planning moment by moment

Think about how you overtake a slow vehicle on the highway. You check that the road is clear. Your mind creates a picture, a scenario, of your completed overtaking manoeuvre. In your mind you have completed the manoeuvre before you start it. Then you accelerate and move out to go around. Each moment while you're overtaking you keep observing forward to determine whether the passing scenario remains intact. No obstacle ahead, keep going. If an obstacle to your overtaking scenario happens, you respond by applying the brakes. The process is open, flexible, and responsive to changes in the scenario.

In essence, each moment you are using feedback that matches the scenario to what is actually happening on the road as the moments pass. Your mind is continually re-picturing the scenario ahead and you adjust your actions accordingly. This allows you to stay in control of the manoeuvre whatever happens.

It's a similar process for profitable trading in markets.

Once you have selected the high-profit scenario and started to engage it in the market you need to be open, flexible and responsive to changes in the scenario. The management imperatives outlined in chapter 2 are continuously integrated with your scenario as it unfolds moment to moment so that you stay in control.

This means using analysis not as prediction but to aid you in the creation of workable, tradeable scenarios based on the information available at any given moment. This kind of analysis is dynamic and harnessed to the action of the market as it unfolds. It has the best chance of putting you in harmony with the market. You'll be long if the market goes up and you'll stay with your purchase if the market keeps going up. If the market goes down, your scenario changes and you respond accordingly.

If you agree with the market you will prosper. You have another A1 method that you can integrate into your feedback process. If your trade is losing you are not in agreement with the market. Get out. If you are in profit, stay in, and even accelerate by loading onto your position, because you are in harmony with the market. Analysis of your profit and loss is an excellent way to gauge and improve your progress.

There is a final point that should be made about the dynamic scenario management I am recommending. The process is intuitive. You don't have to think about it. You don't calculate. Rather you trust your mind's ability to instantaneously and successfully respond to any change in the scenario.

Summary

When you drive your car, you do it intuitively. It will take practice and experience for you to become intuitive in your trading business. The development of this intuition is the hallmark of the Peak Performance Zone. In the same way that you drive your car in the Peak Performance Zone, there is nothing to hold you back from the trading Zone. Or is there?

Profitable traders have the same information base as everybody else. Yet they do well while most don't. Can we blame the market for this? No. For some answers as to why the majority can't trade well, we must examine the psychological speed bumps that hamper performance.

Speed and traffic: psychological barriers and speed bumps

When you take your car out, it's a reasonable expectation that you'll reach your destination. If I asked you to drive from Sydney to Perth, or from Seattle to Denver, you would take out the road map if the route was unfamiliar to you and plan your journey. But you are at your destination in your mind's eye even before you set out. You expect to achieve your outcome — and you do.

Driving from Sydney to Perth or Seattle to Denver is infinitely more dangerous and demanding in terms of constant scenario planning, moment by moment feedback, and execution of driving actions than trading. It requires consistent peak performance.

Why doesn't this ability of intuitive responsiveness behind the wheel translate for most into their trading operations?

The answer's simple, but when you think about it in conjunction with the car analogy, it's astounding. Amazingly, most people don't actually envision their successful outcome in trading. (They might imagine it, in terms of 'winning' lots of cash, but do they envision it—that is, plot the points on the journey, thinking every stage and process through as it happens?)

Is this laziness? Inexperience? Or something else? In the chapters so far I have outlined the cognitive or intellectual demands for success. Now we'll look at the psychological demand—because *your own psychology* can place speed bumps and barriers to your progress and the achievement of your trading journey. I've already given you some indication that the way you think about trading is important; you know that it's necessary to control your emotions, to remain calm, to be able to switch from buying to selling without any emotional attachment. In this chapter, I'll talk about the flip side of this: the self-doubt and internal conflicts that might rear their head, and how to deal with them.

There is an oft-used quote attributed to SuperTrader Ed Seykota on how emotions affect trading:

> *Win or lose, everybody gets what they want from the market. Some people seem to like to lose, so they win by losing money.*

So, referring to figure 4.1, let's look at the impact on behaviour of belief structures, values, internal conflicts and negative self-talk, and how these affect our trading.

Oh, the anxiety!

You already know that your operations in financial markets are shrouded in uncertainty. And, as I pointed out in chapter 2, that that is exactly why you profit. Uncertainty is your friend. But whereas you take the uncertainty in driving your car in your stride, most find the uncertainty in financial markets, the anxiety of not knowing the future, if not crushing, then pretty inhibiting. People are frightened of risk in the market because they don't have enough experience or don't trust their strategies to manage it. Yet they don't worry about these things when they drive a car!

When you drive you have the belief and perception that it is doable because everybody else does it. In trading, however, you *don't* see everybody else doing it properly. It isn't a common experience. In fact, you see a lot of people crashing and burning.

Figure 4.1: observable behaviour

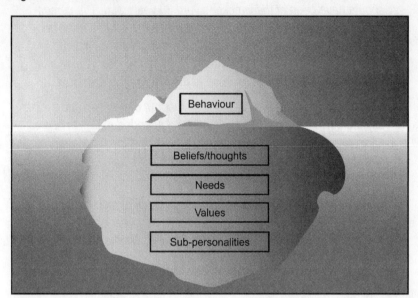

Success in financial markets isn't routine like it is in the driving arena. In fact how many SuperTraders do you know? You may have read books about market wizards and trading 'heroes', but the models offered in the books are impersonal and remote. They are 'out there' and not part of your direct observational experience. In a sense these models could be making the job harder, rather than easier, for you.

Let's not think about the heroes for now, though. Let's concentrate on you. You need to build the internal belief that you will succeed. After all, in life you generally get the results you think and feel you deserve and are capable of.

In trading, some people are beaten before they start. Have a look at an email I received in response to an article I wrote in a trading magazine. Do you identify with and share this view?

I read your article in the last issue of YourTradingEdge ... *[and] one thing doesn't allow me to sleep at night. It is of course the 6 to 7 digit profits some traders make. I have heard that statement before, but I have lost faith that it is possible. Some time ago I was attending an Australian Technical Analysts Association [ATAA] meeting and as I parked a few streets away I saw a man getting out of his vehicle. He was the speaker at the meeting. His vehicle should have been at the wrecker's yard 30 years ago. The person is noted for his articles in trading magazines, he wrote a good book about trading. I have a feeling that many educators are making seminars to make a living; they can't make money from the market. They use ATAA meetings to promote their expensive seminars.*

I have spent the last five years learning about the market and psychology; I have read many books and attended many seminars. I am an active trader; I have no problem with pulling the trigger. I have not made any good money from the market so far and I personally do not know anyone that has.

Can you tell me in percentage terms how much a good trader can make? Is 100 per cent or 200 per cent in every year possible? Those traders with 6 to 7 digit profits, how big are their accounts?

The person who wrote this email, let's call him Steve, raises a whole host of issues and probably contains views that many potential traders hold. This is my reply:

Let me say you just won't break out of the break-even rut if you don't think it is possible. I have a many clients who return six figures and above. But they are people who have decided to be special and do things their own way. Reading books and going to seminars doesn't make money. Your mental edge will, and that's where I come in. I have the knack of taking people from the break-even rut into the superior performance class. If you choose I can help you too. But you have to be prepared to change what you are doing now because if you don't you will continue to achieve the same results, but nothing more.

I can't speak for the motives of other providers. Your observation is possibly apt.

Let's examine some of the issues raised in the initial email.

You will have already spotted the contradiction about the ATAA speaker and his car. A wealthy person is entitled and free to live life any way he or she chooses. A confident and secure person does not need to drive a status symbol although having the means to do so. The presenter's preference may have been to drive his old banger.

What Steve is really saying is that if he were a SuperTrader, then he would drive an expensive car which conforms to his stereotype of success. Presumably the ATAA speaker would be able to drive an expensive car because of the income from his book and the expensive seminars he runs, even if he wasn't a successful trader.

Steve is cynical about trading educators—seminar presenters. If these educators are staking their reputation on a false claim of fortune they've made trading then this is a case of fraud. But Steve seems to be laying a lesser accusation: that the educators are unable to put their money where their mouths are. They talk in terms of theory without having practical experience of becoming and remaining a SuperTrader. If Steve wants to learn from SuperTraders, he'll have to learn to discriminate between the talkers and doers.

It is not the role of the ATAA to make people into SuperTraders. Its role is to educate its members and discuss issues that pertain to technical analysis, one form of analysis that is useful to traders.

In fact, it is a naïve expectation that you might find SuperTraders at the ATAA. The ATAA, the publications, the trading expos, and the seminars are all directed at the public—and the public doesn't have an edge. You won't get your trading licence by these means, even if you are a diligent student. A real benefit of the information and events organisations such as this offer is that they serve as a function for getting people interested. But to really be successful you have to have an edge; in other words you have to be different.

The books, ATAA meetings and the seminars have taken Steve as far as he can go without changing tack. He has been trading for some time and is not losing money. But he is at an impasse; he doesn't have a viable edge. To advance, Steve has to move forward.

The next part of the journey for Steve and others in the break-even rut is a journey within. This journey involves courage, integrity, confidence and the commitment to advance into the unknown; to develop an individual identity and methodology as a trader and then to continue with the process, strengthened by this new edge.

But there is a problem highlighted by the example of Steve that many others are likely to share. It's this: Steve does not have a model for the outcome of his growth. In fact he doesn't believe it is possible because of the limitations of the formative experience he has had so far. This is why he lacks faith that a six-figure income is possible. Steve is asking, 'Show me someone who has done it.' This reassurance might give him the leap of faith required for the next part of his journey.

But as I said to Steve, if he doesn't believe it's possible to succeed then he won't succeed.

Are you like Steve? Do you believe it is possible? Do you believe you will succeed? Are you prepared to master the anxiety associated with trading? Are you prepared to step outside your comfort zone of non-winning ideas and prejudices? Are you prepared to establish and develop an edge and gain your trading licence?

The attainment of your trading licence is a testimony to your personal growth and the power to create your own desires. It shows you are on your way to becoming your own 'hero'.

Two killers: impulsiveness and hesitation

In driving you can be killed or seriously injured even when your vehicle is at rest. It's a very risky enterprise. Excessive speed and inattentiveness can be killers. Alcohol or tiredness might be the cause behind many accidents, but the actual killers are impulses such as impatience and hesitation cropping up at the wrong moment.

Impulsiveness and its antidote

Impulsiveness and its companion, impatience, cause a driver to go too fast for the road conditions or take opportunities that shouldn't be taken. It's your impulsive instincts that suggest you overtake into the traffic flow or ignore the stop sign. It's similar in trading.

Basically, impulsiveness is caused by feeling that you don't want to miss out; you don't want to be left behind. What if everyone else is onto something and you're hanging back? Wouldn't that be terrible!

Impulsiveness and hesitation are potential killers not only on the road but also when trading in financial markets. Both are a response to anxiety felt while trading—an anxiety about the future that manifests itself as a lack of discipline.

You might be itching to enter a trade but nevertheless you have to wait until the scenario offers you the best entry. The market won't move just because you are ready. You are obliged to align your actions to what the market does, not what you want or would like.

This is where being in control of your anxiety helps, because otherwise you might find that your impulsiveness plays a trick on you. You might convince yourself that you see a 'set-up' for an entry when really there isn't one.

Your impulsive side will want you to buy because the price is falling without waiting for an initial confirmation of a rally. It will make you want to buy when prices have been accelerating for some time: it will make you want to join in the froth and bubble of the party even though you arrive late and the party is ready to pack it in. It may even want you to buy on a 'tip', or a press report, as if someone else knows the future. It suggests that you don't have to take responsibility to profit.

Impulsiveness is manifest when you have missed one or two opportunities. It will make you want to play 'catch up' and you will enter another position as if it was a replay of the first or second.

However, what's really happening here is that your impulsiveness is making you unavailable for the random outcomes we saw were essential in chapter 2. If you're listening to the voice in your head saying 'you've got to do this' or 'everyone else is doing that' then you're not actually looking at what is going on in the market. It's a key difference between what you feel and what you see; and market responsiveness will only come about from keen observation.

Another detriment of impulsiveness is your inability to handle the anxiety of the unknowable future. It causes you to close out of a trade soon after entry without confirming it was wrong. Impulsiveness demands you have instant gratification.

The antidote to impulsiveness is patience. Patience is a requirement for successful trading, driving and living. In the market setting, patience—along with insightful and well-planned scenarios—requires of you to wait for the market to confirm your scenarios and then work the flow as the market unfolds.

The curse of hesitation

I think hesitation is more psychologically damaging than impulsiveness. Hesitation and its companion procrastination are caused by the inability to commit because you might be wrong; you might lose. Take the following example.

Say Adele decides not to enter the position at the moment when her scenario's initial 'moment of truth' is confirmed by the market. Although it was her intention to enter then, she says to herself: 'I'd better wait another day just in case'. Avoidance of the pain of possibly being wrong seems far easier than the equal possibility of profit and satisfaction of being right. Then she might wait one more day for definitive confirmation. On the third day it goes up and then she says: 'Gee whiz, I was right again but now it's too late, it's got away. I'll wait for the retracement.' The problem is, though, that retracement (a price movement in the opposite direction to the previous trend) *may not come*. Adele was right in the first place, but wasn't willing to take the risk, and so even though her scenario was correct, she didn't profit. This makes her frustrated, disappointed and impatient.

Hesitation makes you want to wait until the next corner to see if it was possible to overtake when it first looked opportune. Unfortunately, though, the market will move whether you are ready or not. Hesitation's real motive is wishing for the impossible: to know the future before you can act.

Hesitation is rewarded when the market doesn't play out your scenario; you won't lose money. But, on the other hand, if you hesitate, you can't profit when your scenario is right—which it probably will be about half the time.

After entry, another form of hesitation manifests itself in the inability to exit the position when your scenario's stop loss point is reached. You don't allow yourself to get out when you should. Your concern is: 'What if it rebounds after I close out? I'll look silly if that happens.' The price might rebound; you need a scenario for that eventually. But equally the decline could continue into a rout—a disastrous loss. Your hesitation could be very costly. Think about it this way. Would you hesitate to hit the brakes if, when you pull out to overtake another car, you realise that a semitrailer is coming towards you? It's not going to pull over for you, is it?

The problem with hesitation is that after this negative experience of not cutting your loss, you will find yourself even more hesitant to enter a new position. Hesitation amplifies hesitation.

Another form of hesitation is not taking profits from your winners. You have had a star trade and your (forlorn) hope is that it is going on forever. As the winner starts to retreat you don't want to take responsibility for an action that would book a good profit. You can't sell it because you say 'what if it takes off again?' The answer is to collect the profit and then create a scenario for that possible future event that you can enact if it happens. That is, take responsibility. Work with what is and not what might be.

I have an actual example of this to relate to you about a client, Deepak. Deepak's position was $75 000 in profit. The position began to retreat and he prevaricated and eventually closed it out at break-even. How did he feel? He was disappointed, frustrated, and felt self-loathing, because his profits had been lost.

I remained calm. But this is what I said to him: 'Withdraw $75 000 out of your bank and have a look at it. It's a big pile of money. Then would you get a cigarette lighter and start burning $100 bills? Of course you would not. But this is in effect what you did with the foregone profit of that trade. It was your money and you burned it up.' This may seem harsh medicine to you but the message is a deeply important one, and it's one that you need to take on. Hesitation is costly both financially and psychologically.

The antidote to hesitation and procrastination is to execute the management requirement that pertains to your scenario. You need to take responsibility for your own situation and remain in control. You have to work your trading scenario using all the defensive and attacking management skills it suggests. You cannot hesitate to do your job.

Emotions and the moment of truth

The 'moment of truth' is the point at which an action is required. Here is a summary of desirable and undesirable qualities that surround each moment of truth (see figure 4.2 overleaf).

The market will offer you an abundance of opportunities and moments of truth.

Figure 4.2: the moment of truth

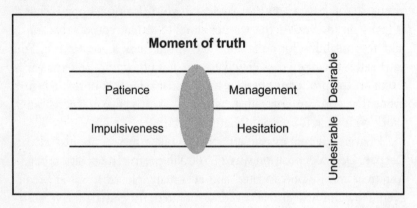

Fear and anxiety

Think back to when you had your first experience of driving a car before you attained your licence. Although you knew driving was possible based on all the other people on the roads, there was still an apprehension in your mind. Can I do it? Will I be able to master the steering wheel, accelerator, brake, gear stick and clutch and be able to drive down the road at the same time? How am I going to reverse park? Do a hill start? Negotiate traffic? Will I crash?

When you do something new it's natural to feel fear. This shouldn't stop you learning, though. Many people have felt afraid when learning to drive; but most of them still kept on learning. And as you learn the operating procedures bit by bit and gradually increase your mastery, you feel less and less fear. Eventually the fear is extinguished and you find that you can do it without inhibition.

Fear is a typical negative response to the anxiety and uncertainty in trading, and it can even play out in your physiology with physical symptoms of anxiety. I'll talk more about these physiological components of fear in the next chapter.

But I want to let you into a secret. Anxiety is a real feature of this business. Nobody can predict the future. In other words, because in this business we are dealing with an unknowable future, there is always anxiety about a particular outcome. SuperTraders accept that fact. They realise that although anxiety is always present, it doesn't have to be feared. In fact, I teach them that anxiety can become an ally to foster sound business practice that is both durable and successful over the long term.

Remember a hit rate of 50 per cent is fine (as long as you work the winners). The secret is that you don't have to have views about the future that you have to defend with your ego. You can release your ego and just deal with the probabilities as they evolve. This enables you to detach from and release the anxiety.

Left by itself, fear will cause bad decisions and bad trading outcomes. It does this in a number of ways:

⇢ Fear makes you take your eyes off the ball.

⇢ It distorts your perception of reality, which can limit your ability to discern a high probability scenario.

⇢ It distorts your ability to implement the actions required by your scenario.

In short. fear inhibits or prevents you from doing your job of stopping losses and working winners.

There is another insidious aspect to fear. It creates a self-fulfilling prophecy: what you fear often happens. If you fear that your account will fall dramatically it probably will. Fear of failure produces the failure that was occupying your mind space.

Below I'll discuss the five specific types of fear that I have observed in my work with clients. These forms of fear all detract from trading success.

Forced awareness

This occurs when a trader (or in this case, let's call him a 'trader' as he's more of a gambler) is forced to close a position with a substantial loss. The stop loss either did not exist or was ignored. The anxiety of holding the loser causes the 'trader' to deny the trade; many will not even review it regularly, saying: 'I'm too busy', or worse still: 'It doesn't matter'. Eventually the pain of holding the loss gets too much and the position is closed out at a much greater loss than if a stop had been used. How often does this signify a market bottom!

The pain and anguish of the loss stays in the memory and can immobilise action so that future trading is impaired. Fear may spiral so that 'trading' gets out of control; or more likely the person gives up, blaming the market, without learning from their mistake. Forced awareness easily escalates fear into a debilitating inability to work with the reality of the market.

Performance anxiety

This applies to those who are unable to enter positions. Although their 'paper trading' results were excellent and despite their best intentions, they are unable to pull the trigger when it comes to actually entering a position with some real money. They can't move from the passenger seat to behind the wheel.

Another incarnation of performance anxiety prevents a trader from pursuing superior returns. This trader uses stops well and can get a winner away, but closes out with only a small profit. He or she does not take the opportunity to load up in order to build the really profitable stake that the moment warrants. The position is closed out early to relieve the pressure of potential success. It belies the truism that you can't go broke taking a profit. Indeed, performance anxiety ensures that you can! Clients in this category consult me for assistance because despite a lot of activity (and not much loss), nothing is gained.

Abandonment fear

Abandonment fear is related to the fear that issues or markets may run and the trader might miss out. As a consequence the trader scans everywhere for opportunities and may end up holding far too many positions to handle. Or the trader may end up with far too much at stake in one position. The end result? The trader may suffer from analysis paralysis. The account is all over the place. Burnout is a possibility. Clients in this category consult me for assistance because of overtrading.

Separation anxiety

Separation anxiety occurs when you have to step outside your comfort zone or perceptions about how the world should operate. It prevents you from taking the next step to growth.

In markets I notice this is a big issue for people who have rigid views about the future, and although aware that the market is acting contrary to their expectations, fail to change their view and act accordingly. Unfortunately I have to tell them that the market is always right and profitability is not a function of one's ego. Instead, it's all about being able to detach from one's own beliefs and see the reality of what the market is actually doing.

Think back to the example that we saw in the section on hesitation. This is a great example of separation anxiety. A trader is in substantial profit and feeling good about it. But the market and the profit begin to retrace. This should be an A1 signal to take at least some profit—but the trader cannot separate from the adage that you let your profits run, and from his good feelings of success that had accumulated as the trade became very profitable. The profits are not running: just the opposite. The end result is that a healthy profit becomes a break-even or a loss trade.

Myopic risk aversion

This occurs when you avoid small risks even when the potential gains far outweigh the losses. It occurs because you are uncertain of the outcome. You think: better to not try because the trade might fail, even though the risk is worth taking. This causes you to enter positions only occasionally, to dabble, to procrastinate.

The best trades are often the 'ugly' ones, the ones with only a tiny hint of confirmation. The risk-averse person will avoid these. This fear ensures that the potential trader will never establish and operate a profitable risk management business.

A new light

I want you look at fear in trading in a new light. Removal of your fear by good practice in driving did not remove the risk. It's still there every time you take the car out. But that's what makes you drive well, makes you maintain constant awareness, and keeps you disciplined on the road. You had to demonstrate that competency to achieve your driver's licence. I want you to turn around your perception of fear in trading in the same way.

Risk won't go away as you become competent—but your fear will, if you allow it to. In fact I want to take this further. Denial of your fear is not desirable or healthy. I want you to acknowledge your fear initially and as you develop competence, and respond by translating any fear into good trading practice. I want you to see fear not as a red light that prevents your progress, but rather as a green light that shows that you are realistically engaging in the management of uncertainty and risk. This attitude is designed to promote good trading, to maintain your awareness of the market, and to retain your discipline. It is designed to advance your quest for profits.

Personality issues: needs and aptitude

We all know about the basic human needs of food, shelter and safety. But in today's world we also know that we consider many other things to be as fundamental or desirable as the basics. Let's call these things needs and desires for a successful life, rather than basic needs. The question is—can successful trading satisfy these important life needs?

Table 4.1 shows a list of higher needs based on those that psychologist William Glasser claimed must be met for a healthy satisfying life.

Table 4.1: higher needs required to lead a satisfying life

Need	Can trading satisfy?
Love and a feeling of belonging	No
Achievement	Yes
Freedom	Yes
Fun	Yes

Trading is a legitimate way to satisfy some deep-seated personality needs. You can't expect trading to make you more lovable or to overcome loneliness. You must satisfy these needs through relationships in your life. But successful trading can and will nourish your sense of achievement, freedom and fun.

You will be able to apply the analysis above to driving. While it's fun, the primary need that causes you to persist with gaining your licence is that of freedom. The thought that you are able to go where you please is a huge motivation.

What is the primary need to be satisfied from your trading project? In my view, you are in this business for achievement. How do we measure achievement in this business? By how much profit you create. It's the profits that are conducive to freedom and fun. When you are successful you can trade from anywhere you like in the world, as long as there is a satellite or cable connection. You are free to dress as you like and you need answer to no-one.

As Ed Seykota said in the quote at the beginning of this chapter, you can lose money and have fun. Casinos after all prefer to present themselves as being in the entertainment industry rather than in the gambling industry.

Say you are achieving well in other areas of life but turn to trading to relieve boredom and frustration. Trading will satisfy these needs without profit. I have clients who come to me and say they aren't interested in the money. They are in it for the challenge (another facet of achievement). That's exactly what they get from the market: challenge, but not profit.

I see that it's possible that you might choose to trade just for fun—but why would you want to do it? Let's come clean. We're in this business to profit, to make money. That's our starting point. Just like when we drive. We do that to go places, too.

People undertake projects in their lives to satisfy needs that are derived in part from heredity and in part from their environment. Satisfaction of needs is very powerful. An unmet need gnaws away unconsciously, causing dissatisfaction and sometimes havoc in our lives.

I have observed that some traders' obvious needs for competition and success are subverted by others such as the need for action in a never-ending event, to be admired as a big-time risk-taker, for sympathy as a loser, for revenge against 'unfair' conditions, to rebel from family expectations, or to escape from the mundane.

Personality mediates and has an impact on the ways we satisfy needs. The way you satisfy your needs is unique and is in line with your personality. And in trading as in life, it is best to act in a way that suits your personality. Not trading in line with your personality may cause you to experience frustration, confusion and boredom.

In my work as a therapist and coach I ask clients questions about their personality aimed at finding out things like:

⇢ where their personality strengths lie

⇢ the pitfalls that particular personality type needs to be aware of in their trading.

Once we have worked through their answers together, I move forward with each client, helping them to build up a picture of the way they will best work in the trading environment.

To do this I use a Personality Needs Profile. Since that could take up a book in itself, here I'll show you the characteristic strengths and weakness of four general personality types. Can you identify yourself?

Traders and investors: the Personality Needs Profile

Type A is the Recognition personality. The strengths and weaknesses of this personality type are as follows.

Strengths:

⇢ drives forward forcefully to achieve recognition as a successful trader

⇢ works better on short-term trends

⇢ is a quick decision-maker

⇢ versatile, able to change tack quickly, can trade long or short.

Weaknesses:

⇢ easily discouraged, wants to be 'right'

⇢ likes to be seen to be doing well

⇢ can put recognition before profit

⇢ is impulsive at times.

Type B is the Social personality. The strengths and weaknesses of this personality type are as follows.

Strengths:

⇢ strong trend follower

⇢ good market listener (goes along with the market)

⇢ successfully implements trading systems developed and used by others.

Weaknesses:

⇢ particularly susceptible to 'market psychology'

⇢ likes to pursue tips and ideas from friends and the media

⇢ slow to recognise trend changes

⇢ likes the 'safety' of the crowd.

Type C is the Security personality. The strengths and weaknesses of this personality type are as follows.

Strengths:

⇢ likes detail

⇢ works hard and consistently towards goals

⇢ doesn't have outlandish expectations, works best with long-term trends

⇢ disciplined in applying an established trading system.

Weaknesses:

⇢ conservative in risk-taking

⇢ needs reassurance from others

⇢ likes to have all the information before taking action

⇢ can be inflexible or be let down by tunnel-vision.

Type D is the Achievement personality. The strengths and weaknesses of this personality type are as follows.

Strengths:

⇢ achievement-oriented, aggressive will to win, competitive

⇢ creative and enthusiastic

⇢ independent

⇢ innovative—likely to develop personal trading ideas and systems.

Weaknesses:

⇢ can fight markets: has a need to prove the market is wrong

⇢ always looking to pick tops and bottoms and so can override trading signals

⇢ personality most likely to make and then lose a fortune.

What rings true for you? Pinning down your Personality Need Type shows you what you are good at and what you should pursue as well as giving you the opportunity to minimise the disruption from your blind spots.

You've got the personality: do you have the aptitude?

Personality is one thing, but do you have the right kind of behaviour and approach? In other words, do you have the aptitude to be a trader?

In my work with clients I use a different profiling system, this time called the DiSC Classic Personal Profile System. This self-report instrument gives you an insight into your trading behaviour. Once we have a good overview I can work with my clients to help them make any changes necessary within themselves. And the aim? To help them become successful traders, of course.

The Personal Profile System asks questions aimed at finding out information such as:

⇢ Does what you do now align with what's required for successful trading?

⇢ What behaviours do you need to change?

⇢ Do you think it's too hard to make these changes?

⇢ And, finally, are you sure you really want to?

When completing the profile it is essential to respond with trading activity as the environmental focus. People behave differently in different environments. Success in the trading environment requires a particular set of behaviours that are pinned down by the instrument.

The Personal Profile System identifies respondents' perception of their immediate environment (in this case, the trading environment) and their perception of their personal power within it. People can be divided up into four behavioural types: dominance, influence, steadiness and conscientiousness. The list below describes attributes of each of these types.

→ *High-intensity dominance* people like action, opportunity and challenges. They are driven by results and control.

→ *High influence* people are talkers who like to get results through people. They are driven by people involvement and recognition.

→ *High steadiness* people are team players who always meet deadlines. They are driven by security and stability.

→ *Highly conscientious* people are sticklers for detail who like to operate under known standards and written instructions. They are driven by accuracy and order.

The market environment is unfavourable. A trader has to accept having no control over the market; indeed a trader has only perceptions of the market to work with. These perceptions can only approximate the market, and never fully and consistently encapsulate it. So it's fair to say that having the aptitude to be a successful trader is not about whether or not you'll be able to control the market. It's all about whether you have the personal beliefs and skills to accept complete responsibility for your actions and equity. You need to be in control and know that you have the power to act on your own behalf as necessary.

So what is the ideal behaviour-set for success as a trader based on the Personal Profile System? Did you guess correctly? The ideal dimension for a trader or investor is high intensity dominance.

The ideal trader or active investor

An idea trader or active investor has the following characteristics:

→ emphasises shaping the environment by overcoming opposition and challenges

→ tends to get immediate results, take action, make quick decisions

⇢ is motivated by new and varied challenges, opportunity for accomplishment, personal power and authority

⇢ fears loss of control, being taken advantage of

⇢ is self-confident, decisive and a risk-taker

⇢ is limited by impatience, the desire to move forward without considering outcomes.

I use the Personal Trading Profile to show my clients their aptitude for trading. The results show you have the behavioural platform to reach your goals to be a successful trader if you are strong-willed, decisive, efficient, versatile, competitive, independent and practical.

If, as a high-intensity dominance person, your fear is triggered, you may overuse your strength and act negatively and defensively. Under these conditions you may become overconfident, pushy, impatient, indiscriminate, attacking and harsh. You should be alert for these attributes under pressure and work towards your positive qualities at all times.

If your Personal Trading Profile reveals high intensity influence, steadiness or conscientiousness, the news is good. Unlike personality, behaviour is flexible and dynamic; you can adapt. You can do one of three things:

⇢ Learn to use new behaviours to speed up your journey to consistent profitability.

⇢ Keep going as you are and let market experience force the changes upon you.

⇢ Choose put the appropriate adaptations in the 'too hard basket', give up your trading aspirations, find a good fund manager and enjoy your life in other ways.

It's the same as when you are working towards gaining your driver's licence. The appropriate aptitude for trading successfully is a necessary requirement, but not the only one. It's eminently possible to reach the appropriate aptitude through a combination of learning and experience. Remember: if you were willing to put the work into learning to drive well, you have the ability to learn how to profit in financial markets too.

What holds 'traders' back?

There's a saying that I think is just as true in trading as it is in life: you can't consistently behave in ways that are inconsistent with your own beliefs.

Assuming that most people come to trading with the conscious expectation that they will profit handsomely through their activity, why is it that most don't achieve this expectation? Or why do some achieve success but then fail to continue with it?

To answer these questions, we have to delve further into the psyche and psychology of the potential trader.

There are many burdens that prevent people achieving their desires. I've looked at fear and its debilitating effects, and addressed the question of needs satisfaction; that is, whether you are going about the task in a way that will satisfy your unique personality needs. I've talked about delving into the aptitude of a potential trader to see if it lives up to the requirements of the task. Now it's time to move on to a critical barrier to success: misbeliefs.

Logically you can see the problem. I'll give you an example. Maria expects and intends to win, as any rational trader should. She translates that intention into effort and action. But if Maria doesn't win then there is a very strong chance that she doesn't really believe deep down that winning is possible. Or perhaps she believes that winning is possible for others, but that she doesn't deserve to win, or that she just isn't a 'winner'.

Maria's conscious desire to win is subverted by her subconscious and very powerful misbeliefs about how to obtain and sustain success. In essence what she consciously strives for and what she really believes are incongruent. Her misbeliefs win out.

What are some of the misbeliefs that hold traders back from success? Let's now take a look at some specific misbeliefs as they pertain to markets, analysis and the individual trader.

Misbeliefs about the market

One key subconscious misbelief relates to the way traders perceive their market operations.

A trader may hold and act on the misbelief that speculation is essentially gambling, and that the outcome depends on luck or a fluke. As you know, the *truth* is that speculation in markets is a business: a special business of handling risk in the light of uncertainty about the future. Because of the uncertainty it may seem like gambling but taking a businesslike approach to uncertainty means managing that risk to your advantage. A gambler takes a position about the future and that's it. A speculator takes a position and keeps realigning it with the market as it unfolds. A speculator with a business orientation will cut losing positions and when a position agrees with the market direction will not only stay with it but also add to it.

A second misbelief about markets follows on from the first. Many potential traders are beaten before they start because they falsely believe that winning in the face of uncertainty is not possible or even that because they can't win, nobody wins. People with this misbelief need to accept that it is possible to win with a detached, disciplined and responsive approach. Some of my clients do extremely well with six- or seven-figure annual returns. The challenge for these SuperTraders—as it is for traders at any level—is to keep stretching and growing; to maintain and strengthen their edge.

Successful market speculators get very well paid. This leads to further misbeliefs that trading is parasitic or that speculators gain their money too easily. Nothing could be further from the truth. The proficient speculator buys low when the risk of buying is unacceptable for most and sells high when the risk for most seems to have abated, or conversely sells high and buys low. The successful speculator takes frequent high-level risks. Not only this, but they do this consciously and based on their experience and knowledge. You don't get something for nothing—and successful speculation is hard work. If you have a misbelief that speculation is easy you may end up sabotaging your outcomes by not bothering to put in the hard work yourself.

Misbeliefs about analysis

When I put the word analysis here many of you will automatically read the subtext as technical analysis. Herein lies one of the misbeliefs about analysis: because technical analysis involves complex computer-derived quantitative algorithms, it's often thought that there must be an associated superiority if not infallibility about it. This is a naïve view.

All analysis you conduct is subjective, in the sense that you select and apply the analytical criteria to pump into the algorithm. The same applies to quantitative fundamental analysis: it is arbitrary too. I have clients who are successful with technical analysis, fundamental analysis and an amalgam of both. As you know, I'm certainly not a fan of treating analysis as gospel. What I encourage my clients to do is to use the information about what the market is doing now—the analysis—to create tradable probability scenarios in the future. Some of my most successful clients are entirely intuitive traders.

There is only one piece of truth and that is what the market actually does. If your analysis agrees with the market then it is successful—*on this occasion*. This is no guarantee that it will be successful next time.

Another misbelief is that there is an analytical 'Holy Grail' or big secret that explains everything and is a universal predictor. Analysts spend hours, and some a lifetime, in trying to elicit such a formula. There isn't one, and if there was one, the market would soon respond to it by discounting it. Think back to the poker example in the previous chapter. It simply isn't true that in markets the future is always an extrapolation of the past. Markets are ever-changing in the way they go up, down and sideways. A successful speculator works analyses early and, with limited information about what the change probably is, creates a scenario, and then goes for it.

Analysis is one tool in the box for success. It's a misbelief to think that trading is just applied analysis. Many think this is true and search for the guru or system that will never fail them. Of course analysis can be useful, but it is only a small if necessary part of the winning story.

Personal misbeliefs

Personal misbeliefs are the specific falsehoods that prevent you from achieving your desires. Each trader brings unique misbeliefs to bear on his or her trading outcomes. These derive from the formative life experiences, value structure and negative self-talk that lurk well below the surface of conscious thought but which subliminally direct our behaviour.

Here's an example: 'I'm a Smith, and Smiths have always been badly burned by markets. Look what happened to Grandad in 1929. He lost everything.' This person's subconscious expectation and self-talk set them up for failure because it embodied a personal misbelief that family history automatically repeats.

In my work I have come across many different personal misbeliefs. One common one is: 'every time I trade I put myself on the line.' Now this may reflect insecurity about money but the intrinsic problem here is one of ego. It's very important for this trader to be right, and right all the time. When not right, and you can be wrong more than half the time and still do very well, this trader feels disappointed, hurt and even betrayed. These factors are not conducive to taking your next trade and doing the job properly.

When you enter a trade you are only risking a predetermined amount of money that you are willing to back your judgement with. It is part of the series of moves that your business plan calls for. I certainly steer my clients away from personal attachment to individual trades because successful trading is a business like any other, rather than an outlet for ego gratification. And how do you ensure that you don't feel that you're 'putting yourself on the line'? It's simple. Make sure that you are comfortable with the amount of money you're putting up. Keep the amounts small.

There is a misbelief that prevents traders who become successful from really going on with it. This misbelief is that there is a ceiling for success which can't be penetrated. I have a client who for several years had made $3 million a year as a proprietary trader. He would rapidly reach this figure and bump against it but could not exceed it. Working together, we have linked the fact that he *has* the capacity to break the ceiling with the appropriate belief structure to enable him to actually do it.

There are plenty of other personal misbeliefs. In fact there are as many as there are traders. Here are a few more and of course you can add your own.

→ a catastrophe is imminent

→ I'm a victim of market-makers and manipulators

→ when I'm successful at trading I'll earn more love and respect

→ small accounts are forced to dabble

→ only the 'big boys' win

→ the market is wrong, I'm right

→ the market is against me

→ I can only enter a position when it feels good

→ markets are unfathomable

→ intraday traders can't succeed.

Dealing with misbeliefs

Remember the statement: *you can't consistently behave in ways that are inconsistent with your beliefs*. On the surface the answer to misbeliefs is to replace them with true beliefs to facilitate your success. You can be sure that successful traders whom you are operating against have identified, come to terms with, and overcome their misbeliefs. That's why they are successful.

When not successful, most people, if they don't give up, turn to external remedies to look for improvement. Some of these remedies are to find another guru, work harder on the analysis, attend another course to find out the 'secret', or tinker with their trading system. While some gains can be made here, the truth is that for real and lasting improvement, change has to be internal: within the cognitive set and psyche of the trader. This is why coaching from a qualified professional is so important.

Don't let yourself be conned into expensive superficial solutions when the answers are already within you. Furthermore, don't subject yourself to the misbelief that you are unworthy of receiving personal help or that it is a sign of insecurity or weakness. Instead, view it as a sign that you do want to do well and are prepared to undertake the necessary personal growth to secure your desires from trading in the future.

What values are important for a successful trader?

I am using the word values in a psychological sense rather than a monetary sense. Values are default ideas from which we unconsciously operate our lives. The *Concise Oxford Dictionary* defines a value in this context as: 'one's principles or standards, one's judgement of what is valuable or important in life'.

Our behaviour is a reflection of our values.

Professionalism

A key value that I think is important for trading success is that of professionalism. Yes—I want you to be financially remunerated for your trading activity. But professionalism goes much further than this.

Professional people have a particular *modus operandi* as well as a keen interest (if not devotion and passion) in their chosen field. Professionals have a commitment to self-improvement and learning. They have an edge which is always being developed.

Professionals follow procedures that they creatively adapt to suit each situation as it confronts them. Furthermore they completely detach from their own needs and ego while they immerse themselves in their task. They don't think of the money while they are performing. In other words they use their reservoir of experience to do whatever it takes to achieve the best outcome at each moment.

You don't want the heart surgeon to open your chest and then lose confidence or become impulsive or hesitant. Years of guided practice and experience ensures that she doesn't.

The heart surgeon has done all the technical analysis beforehand: ultrasound, X-rays, ECGs and blood tests, but when the incision is made she goes to work and uses all her skill to solve this specific problem with poise and confidence. If she planned to do a double bypass but realises that a triple is needed after examining the heart during the operation, does she just do the double because that was her rigidly held view? No: as a professional she does what is required in the moment. She is committed to the best outcome possible in a non-attached yet deliberate way. She expects to succeed.

Another point can be made here. Think how heart surgery has changed over the last 20 years. Heart surgeons as professionals do not apply procedures uniformly irrespective of particular patient needs. They don't expect to find the rule or 'Holy Grail' that can be stuck to rigidly forevermore. Professional people are always looking to become more efficient by evaluating what they do with a view to doing it better and better. In other words professionals are open to improvement through feedback from their own activity.

To be consistently successful you must implement the value of professionalism. Your trader's licence is just the first step on a lifelong journey towards being a fully professional trader.

Prosperity

The second key value necessary for successful trading is that of prosperity.

Is the glass half full or half empty? Neither: it is overflowing with opportunity and abundance. I believe financial markets were created to be a vehicle for our financial prosperity. This isn't just positive thinking; it's a core value.

Most people are encultured to think lack and scarcity is the norm. They are taught that money isn't nice, that it's a necessary evil. Even so, rich or poor, it's good to have money. Unfortunately a poverty consciousness pervades society. If you share this you won't profit in markets and if you do you will either sabotage or not enjoy your rewards.

Typically the poverty consciousness encourages us to resent people who do well, especially financially, and see them as being immoral or greedy. As Michael Douglas's character Gordon Gekko says in the film *Wall Street*:

> *The point is, ladies and gentleman, that greed—for lack of a better word—is good. Greed is right. Greed works. Greed clarifies, cuts through and captures the evolutionary spirit. Greed, in all of its forms—greed for life, for money, for love, for knowledge—has marked the upward surge of mankind.*

These famous words reveal a common value that the only way to success is through selfish greed and sharp practice. Ironically this value is actually conducive to disappointment and/or failure in trading financial markets. Replace the word 'greed' with the word 'profit' or 'ambition' or 'commitment' or 'responsibility', and then it works.

Being profitable at trading is not the result of greed. It's the result of the operation of a professionally run, competitive and legitimate business. It's the result of a prosperous value set that expects success and achieves it.

I recommend to my clients that as a sign of their prosperity they unobtrusively give away 10 per cent of their profits to an organisation or individual which does good in society or which is a source of inspiration to them. If you're thinking 'what a waste' then scarcity is probably your prime value. If you think and know that money you give away comes back to you tenfold or more, then prosperity is your driver. It shows that are you comfortable with money. It shows you are indeed open to the rich abundance of this world, and to financial markets.

Your hidden sub-personalities

Only one thought can hold sway in our conscious mind at any one time. So when you approach trading, where do thoughts like 'better not, you might lose' or 'you don't deserve to win' come from? Where does the negative self-talk that leads to impulsiveness, hesitation and failure come from?

These thoughts come from deep in our unconscious mind and they have been there for a long, long time.

In the unconscious mind there are sub-personalities or entities that, left unattended, have a potentially huge negative impact on what we do. They create conflict and incongruity between what we plan in our conscious mind, what we do and what we end up achieving.

Here are a few common ones that have surfaced in my work with trading clients—all feelings of self-doubt and worthlessness:

⇢ you're not worthy

⇢ you're just selfish

⇢ you are inadequate for the task

⇢ you don't know enough

⇢ you need protection

⇢ you're getting above yourself

⇢ you are definitely going to fail

⇢ you'll never succeed

⇢ what makes you think you're so smart?

⇢ this isn't possible.

And you may be able to add one or two your own.

I do a lot of work with traders in this area. We work non-judgementally. We assume these entities are neither bad nor good. They're just there and may have in fact been useful previously in your life. What we aim to do is understand their intent and then take them on a journey into your super-conscious state. This is the state of mind wherein we are powerful, responsive, decisive, creative, intuitive, poised, and responsible. The state also is characterised by love, especially self-love, generosity and altruism.

What we do is transform the negativity associated with the sub-personality into a positive force that enhances our trading success. This transformation works wonders for traders. It is liberating. Worked with properly, the very thing that is limiting you can be synthesised into a powerful asset to help you secure your success.

Among other methods, I use meditations, creative visualisation and psychosynthesis strategies in this quest.

Summary

As I said in the introduction to this book, you have already experienced the Zone, or this super-conscious state, many times in your life. This is the state in which you drive your car. Despite all the speed-bumps and psychological obstacles mentioned in this chapter, you need to know that you do have the ability to secure your trading profits.

Next, I'll discuss the development of the peak performance skills—the activity aspect of profitable trading.

Driving processes
and skills

In this book I suggest that many of the processes and skills you use to safely and effectively drive your car are similar to those needed in your quest for consistent trading profit. Whereas you are completely at home in managing the far greater risk when you drive, until you develop a similar level of ease and skillfulness through practice, your trading experience will feel awkward. To secure your trader's licence you need to possess the full repertoire of trading skills and show that you have the ability to apply them in a real 'road test'.

The processes and skills required to achieve your licence are not innate for the vast majority of people; rather, they are very much learned behaviours. This is the good news. The bad news is that they aren't natural at first; in fact they are quite uncomfortable and challenging. But just as in driving, you can learn the skills so well that you come to operate them without needing to think about it—in other words, you'll be able to operate in the Zone.

So what specific skills and processes are mandatory for success in driving your trading behaviour car?

Your trading behaviour car

When we look at human behaviour as a whole, it is composed of four elements:

⇢ physiology

⇢ emotions

⇢ thinking

⇢ doing.

These elements go with you everywhere.

Let's use a car as a metaphor for behaviour (see figure 5.1). The four wheels of the car represent the four elements of behaviour. Physiology and emotions are the back wheels, and thinking and doing are the front wheels. When all the elements are functioning in harmony and with purpose, then car will work optimally—or, to think about you instead of the car for one moment, the outcomes of your total behaviour are optimal. This is when you are ready to perform in the Peak Performance Zone.

Figure 5.1: dimensions of behaviour

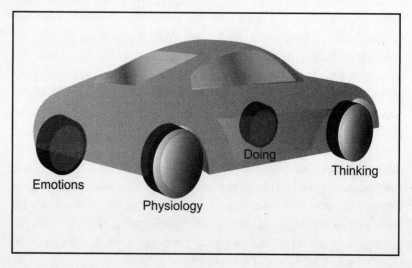

However more is required to enter and sustain trading in the Zone. You have to take responsibility for the journey. You have to make the appropriate choices to integrate the four elements with your goals: to focus on trading for profit; to flawlessly execute your scenario each time. You have to choose to be in complete control of your trading car whatever happens. You have to do what you need to do in the market traffic: you must be alert at all times.

Balance is important in life. You know the outcome when people negotiate their lives primarily on their emotions; it's like trying to drive their car from the back seat. Likewise, you can't drive your trading car from the back seat. You have to hop in the driver's seat, take the steering wheel and take control. And keep driving.

No matter where you're sitting, though, the car won't run without all four wheels. Let's examine each of the four elements in turn to see how they apply to you.

Physiology for the Zone

Needless to say you shouldn't trade when you are ill or intoxicated. But the impact of physiology on your trading edge is quite subtle, so much so that it is mostly overlooked.

The speed with which markets can move, as well as their unpredictable nature, can cause the physiological symptoms of anxiety to manifest. In this state you are likely to be breathing from the top of your chest; you might have sweaty palms; excessive adrenalin could be flowing. And you won't be in the Zone because you will be unable to perform optimally.

The anxiety arises from the fact that your brain is not functioning as it should be. Here your activity is being directed via the centre that controls emotions or even the 'fight/flight' centre in your hind-brain. This is the emergency centre that is activated when you have a near miss in your car for example. It is not desirable to sustain your trading operations in this state. Not only will you make poor quality decisions but also you will burn out!

You can and should be physiologically calm, centred and relaxed to be in the Zone. I think it's important for traders to be generally fit and healthy—it's a positive starting point. I do a program of physiological relaxation with my clients to centre them. This includes deep rhythmic breathing, progressive muscle relaxation and release meditation. Furthermore, I teach clients how to monitor their own physiological state through the trading day so as to determine whether they are in the Zone and, if not, how to re-anchor themselves into the desirable state. As a guideline, you should be as physiologically composed at your trading desk as you are at the steering wheel.

Emotions and peak performance

There is a lot of misinformation about the role that emotions play in trading.

In September 2005 a Reuters report titled 'Wanted: psychopaths to make a killing in markets' was published. The article outlined research that shows 'functional psychopaths'—people who have sustained damage to their brain causing emotional impairment, or those who are just unemotional—make good financial decisions when handling high risk:

> *In a study of investors' behaviour 41 people with normal IQs were asked to play a simple investment game. Fifteen of the group had suffered lesions on the brain that affect emotions. The result was that those with brain damage outperformed those without.*

While the tone of the article was somewhat tongue-in-cheek, it revealed a misbelief about emotions in trading: that you can only be successful when you don't have emotions.

The truth is that emotions go with you everywhere. You can't, unless you have brain damage or are psychopathic, not have emotions. Your emotions will cease when your heart stops beating. Denial of your emotions is unproductive and unhealthy.

So the question arises: how do you become successful if you do have to acknowledge your emotions?

Successful trading is first and foremost a doing activity. You do things, that is, manage, to work your winners and cut your losers. There's no reason that you can't acknowledge your emotions and still perform correctly. The important thing is not to let the emotion distract you from the actions and tasks that are imperative for your success.

Think of your emotions as backseat drivers. There's no reason not to listen to them, but remember that you're the one in control of the steering wheel. It's up to you to operate sound strategies that will make you profitable. You need to be able to do things that don't feel good emotionally. A jumbo jet pilot can't say: 'I'm not landing the plane today because I don't feel like it.' Professional people are able to sufficiently detach themselves from their negative emotions to perform well. Surprisingly, the distracting negative emotions gradually transform into positive ones that are associated with their success.

Because trading involves the management of risk and uncertainty people tend to automatically default to the negative emotions of fear and anxiety. Often rational actions are distorted by the 'fright and flight' response that these emotions produce. In this sense, I agree with the sentiments of the Reuters article. Fear and anxiety create poor trading outcomes. But the way to move forward is to control your emotions, not eradicate them. One way to deal with your emotions is to transform the negative emotions of fear and anxiety into positive ones such as calmness, confidence, gratitude, presence and self-belief. An emotional lobotomy is not required!

There are other negative emotions as well as fear which can subvert profitable trading outcomes. The emotions associated with complacency, greed and entitlement also take you out of the Zone. Never think that the market will pay you just because you turn up and trade. You are not entitled to profit because you have been on a course, have a coach, or because you have been profitable in the past. Each moment in the market is a fresh one requiring your diligence and commitment to best practice.

In the same Reuters article, Professor Baba Shiv of the Stanford Graduate School of Business is quoted as stating that emotions serve an adaptive role in speeding up decision-making. Nevertheless he claims the natural yet negative emotions associated with risk inhibit wise decisions.

So if we can replace uninhibited negative emotions with the positive purposeful ones indicated in figure 5.2 (overleaf) we allow not only faster but also better trading decisions.

Figure 5.2: the desirable emotion wheel

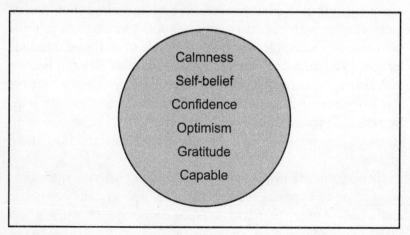

Calmness
Self-belief
Confidence
Optimism
Gratitude
Capable

Thinking: intuition for peak performance

I want to point out here a limitation in the conventional thinking about trading. Most people approach trading as if it is a left-brained, analytical, reductionist, and quantitative activity. It is understandable that this is the case because our education systems promote left-brained thinking as the only avenue to success. However I think that right-brain activity is not only legitimate but also essential for consistent success.

The right brain is the qualitative, creative side that looks for connection and anomaly. Using all your brain capacity, left and right, makes sense.

The outcome of whole-brain thinking, that is, integrating the left and right sides, is intuition. Now intuition is not impulsiveness, wishful thinking—or an emotion. It is a way of dealing with information that is always in a state of flux. It means that you are able to process the information flow instantaneously to implement an appropriate response. If you think that sounds like how you drive your car you're right.

Your intuition is the basis for the development of your high-profit probability scenarios. If the evidence changes in the next moment, your intuition will be cognisant of the change and you will be able to adjust your scenario. Intuition is flexible, open, responsive and accurate.

I think the development of genuine intuition is an important aspect of thinking in the Peak Performance Zone. The SuperTraders I know and work with are intuitive thinkers. Because the practice of intuitive thinking is typically not thought highly of, it may take time for you to develop and trust it. But when you do it will transform your trading outcomes.

To summarise this section, here are some affirmations that may benefit your thinking. You need to *think* and affirm:

⇢ I will do my job as a trader: I will profit.

⇢ I will create and manage high-profit probability scenarios.

⇢ I will obtain my licence to trade.

⇢ I am in complete control of my trading.

⇢ I take complete responsibility for my trading account.

⇢ I always do what each scenario's 'moments of truth' require.

⇢ I flick losers with ease.

⇢ I am willing to pay my rent.

⇢ There are plenty of opportunities for me; I am patient.

⇢ The market tells me what to do; my intuition keeps me in harmony with it.

⇢ This trade is just one of many.

⇢ I work my winners to the full.

⇢ I am on my way to becoming a SuperTrader.

⇢ I act like a SuperTrader now.

Doing peak performance: the trading verbs

You can sit in your car, feel relaxed and think: 'Gee, it would be nice to go somewhere, to travel.' But it won't happen just because you think about it or have a look at a road map. You have to do it. A doing word is a verb. The verb for doing in the car context is, of course, 'to drive'. To get somewhere you have to execute driving actions. The corresponding verb in the financial market context is 'to trade': to make profits you have to execute trading actions.

Above all else, this business is a doing one. You have to drive your trading car in order to profit. Just like driving your car, one trading action is followed by another in a continuous flow of appropriate actions as the future unfolds.

Because of the constant variation in the information flow the market presents, there are a set of management verbs that are imperative to execute appropriately.

Being 'flat', or not in a position, is appropriate if there are no opportunities available. On the other hand it is irrational not to enter as indicated by a high probability scenario. Entries are limited to high probability positions in line with your scenario that is aligned with the market flow.

Remember what we saw in chapter 1: once you have entered a position your role has automatically converted to that of vendor. You have to be ready to implement this role.

Another term for scenario is 'anticipatory set'. As we saw in chapter 3, your scenario needs to project forward and anticipate what you do next as new information becomes available. Your scenario is continuously in step with the market. You are always looking for evidence to predicate your next action.

Any time after you initiate a position it can either win or lose, and the trader acts according to whether the market accepts or rejects the position. This is how you *manage* your trading business. You manage by executing your trade with anticipation, timeliness and detachment.

You need to align your positions with what the market is doing more or less continuously. Your scenario enables this. Similarly in driving your car there is a continuous flow of actions dictated by the road and traffic conditions. You take your foot off the accelerator or touch the brakes to slow down as a defensive or safety measure. But when the road is clear you also change gears and put your foot down to get ahead. The degree of action is again determined by the road and traffic conditions.

Similarly there are trading verbs for defence and verbs for attack (see table 5.1). The defensive verbs are aimed at protecting your capital. The attacking verbs are to make your capital grow by focusing on working your profitable trades.

Table 5.1: trading verbs

Enter	
Defensive actions	**Attacking actions**
Scratch	Re-enter
Cut	Hold
Reduce	Take
	Reverse
	Add (load up)

The trading verbs involve precision with defence and attack to maximise returns. At any time you are poised to execute a preplanned defensive or attacking action that your scenario indicates. Your moments of truth are anticipated and you have a verb ready to execute in the next moment if required, synchronised with what the market does.

Including 'enter' there are only nine verbs. Not as complex as in many other professions. Yet there is complexity and subtlety in the permutations and combinations the market requires of you in order to profit.

The defensive verbs

Let's have a look at the defensive verbs. These are our 'brakes' that protect our capital and our profit as it accumulates in a trade. Like driving we have to be ready to apply the brakes at any time, yet we won't get far if all we do is use the brakes.

A trade can be *scratched* after it is entered even before it touches the predetermined stop loss price point. A trade is not scratched because you are unable to weather the uncertainty you experience after entry. Scratching is a legitimate action if, after entry, the scenario that you entered on is no longer apt. You might be in a news-event based trade and some fresh news can alter the scenario, or perhaps your scenario required a quick move that isn't happening.

I deliberately use the word *cut* instead of stop loss. I don't want you thinking loss; remember you must pay rent no matter what. Cutting is the vendor action you unequivocally execute at the price point you predetermined at entry which indicates the position would be wrong. When you see a red light while driving, you would hit the brakes and stop. When your trading scenario flags a red light, you cut. With a 50 per cent hit rate, you will cut half the time. Be grateful that the market has readily told you where not to proceed so that you can put your energy into where you can proceed.

Remember you need to trail your defence up behind the profit as it grows, but not so tightly that you don't give the trade room to move. You have to leave some room for the grey areas to resolve.

Reduce is a defensive strategy that enables you to book some profit when you have made considerable profit. Ironically I am going to show you details of the process when we review the attacking Add verbs.

The attacking verbs

Let's now review the attacking verbs. Indeed we will spend more time focusing on and discussing these. Newcomers and people in the break-even rut find them difficult to put into play. But these are the actions that make you the money.

Re-entry is a very powerful verb. Remember that timing the market perfectly every time is an unrealistic expectation. An occupational hazard of speculation is being too early. Furthermore, the business is founded on the fact that each trade is an independent event. So you have just had to cut a trade. It's over, finished, done. Release it. Look forward to your scenario's next legitimate entry signal and don't hesitate if the opportunity arises. Look forward through the windscreen to determine what you do, not backwards through the rear vision mirror. In fact, as a matter of course it is good procedure when you have just cut a trade to automatically develop a re-entry scenario—it keeps your mind proactive and ready to harness the next opportunity.

It seems strange that I have to remind you to *hold* your position when your trade proves that it is profitable. People seem to be hard-wired to vend when they have a small profit. It's like putting the brakes of the car on just when you are gaining some speed.

Winning trades possess their own tension. In the market the price of a position at each moment in time, not just at entry, is always surrounded by uncertainty. There is a temptation to say: 'What if it comes back against me?' and pre-empt this uncertainty with an unjustified sale. While the trade is profitable then you must hold it, albeit with your defensive stop trailing behind. Because it's equally probable that it might keep going.

It seems strange that I have to include *take* as a trading verb. When the party is over there is no purpose in hanging around. Take your profit. Remember at some stage you have to be a vendor. You don't want to leave profit on the table for it to leak away.

I emphasise taking for those who think that just raising your defensive stop is good enough. Trailing defensive stops is good practice in case the unexpected happens. However for outlier trades there can be some distance from the defensive position, such as the last swing low, and the current market price.

Taking is the best part of the business. A note of warning here: you don't take just because you feel like it. As with all these actions, take has to be part of your scenario plan.

Reverse is the hallmark of versatility and flexibility. You may be aligned with the market going in one direction. But if it changes direction you have to flip your scenario despite your view and recent experience. Remember in the market each moment is independent; each moment something new can happen. If the market gives you information that it has changed direction, then you must too. If there is a bend in the road, heed it!

When you are driving if you see clear road you put your foot down. In trading we *add*, or *load up*. Remember you never add to a loser. When you are on a winner it makes sense to load up, although it is difficult to do. It's loading up on winners that really makes the business lucrative. It elevates your edge ratio without taking on more new trades. Your focus is on maximising the return on those trades that are really good winners.

Let me show you why. To do this we need to refer to the results of the symbols trade simulation in chapter 2. Remember we achieved a hit rate of 52 per cent and an edge ratio of 2. In that experiment we did not load up on any positions. We had 24 + and two ★. What would result if we loaded up on 20 per cent of the winners?

This time let's assume that we load up on a third of the + and receive double the original profit on these. So one-third of the + are worth three units. Similarly every second ★ achieves double the original profit, that is, 12 units.

The hit rate stays exactly the same. But the new edge ratio is greatly improved.

$$ER = [(16 \, +) \times 1.5] \text{ plus } [(8 \, +) \times 3] \text{ plus } [(1 \star) \times 6]$$
$$\text{plus } [(1 \star) \times 12] \text{ divided by } [(24 - \text{and } \cdot) \times 1]$$

The edge ratio produced by loading up calculates to be 2.75.

These assumptions are very conservative. However it shows you the benefit of adding to your winners. Profit escalated from 100 per cent to 175 per cent on risk, and you didn't have to make any fresh entries. I repeat this is without taking more initial trades: you handled your existing ones more efficiently. Now you can see why it is possible to achieve superior returns with a hit rate less than 50 per cent. Now you can see why clients of mine can achieve and sustain edge ratios of six to eight.

The real money in this business is in the adding.

Of course, it is possible that you can add to a winning position and have it suddenly reverse on you. That's why loading up requires you to maintain an immaculate defence. Here is a case where attack and defence especially go hand in hand. You are now driving your car at speed.

When should you load up? Never on a loser, and only on a winner when you can raise your stop. In fact if you can raise your defensive stop you should be automatically considering a loading up scenario.

I want to show you four generic models for loading. Three are attacking and one is quite defensive. On each of the diagrams the price of the instrument continues up as shown on the left-hand vertical axis. The horizontal axis shows how the position size is altered as the price escalates.

Again I stress that the defensive cut line is raised as the position is added to and the price increases. After the first couple of adds this can lock in profit. But remember the reason we load up is not to make small profits but big ones if the market really moves.

Figure 5.3 shows what I call what 'linear loading' because an equal-sized position is bought each time. Figure 5.4 shows the impact of loading less each time.

Figure 5.3: linear loading up

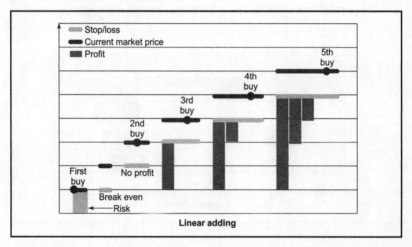

Figure 5.4: loading less

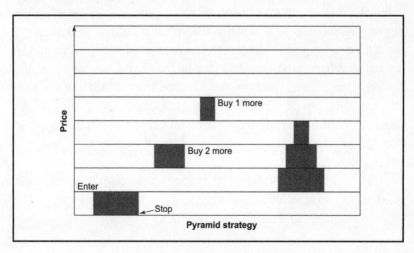

This is a little more conservative than linear loading, and is often called 'pyramiding' because of the shape of the position that is built. It's quite appropriate for an active investment strategy. However it is a strategy that requires a hit rate well above 50 per cent because you take the biggest position first. Compare it with figure 5.5, which shows the impact of loading more each time.

Figure 5.5: loading more

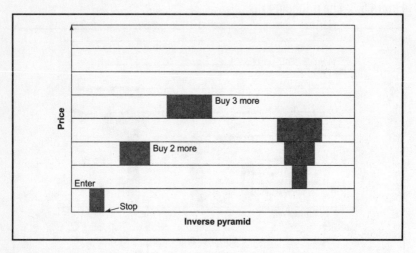

Loading more is not a conservative strategy. It is definitely a strategy for an experienced professional. It requires assiduous and very nimble defence. It has advantages however. You can put a small tester in the market rather than your usual full level of entry risk and see how the market takes it. If it doesn't work, you have found out about the market and have paid very little for it. But if you are right and the market takes off then you can quickly load into a really big position and see some big profits pretty rapidly. It's particularly suitable for those who like to identify reversals and for those who have a low hit rate. (If you had a very high hit rate it would make more sense to start off big.)

Figure 5.6 shows a defensive strategy. It is often proposed, for good reason, as a preferred method for the public. The essence of the strategy is to take a full position at entry and reduce it as the price goes higher to cover trading expenses and to lock in some profit.

Figure 5.6: unloading

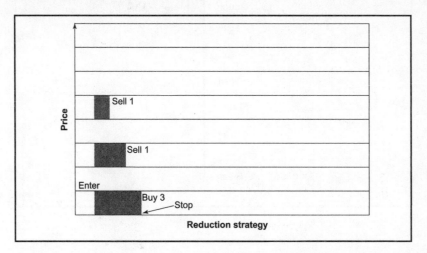

This strategy is appropriate if you get into the position late, as the public often does, and if you need a small profit to maintain your psychological poise.

This is a good way to lock in profit after a lengthy move. It is also an appropriate strategy for intraday 'jobber' trading professionals.

The downfall of a reduction strategy after entry is that if you have a genuine star trade you will limit the potential profit. This unloading strategy is suitable if you have a hit rate well above 60 per cent. It is a poor strategy if you have a low hit rate because you are exposed to the biggest position at first and when you are on a winner you start reducing it.

The 'road' conditions for a trader are the continuous market auction. Given that defence is always required if the auction reverses (which it could do at any time), what form of action is most suitable as the auction progresses in a specific direction? Figure 5.7 (overleaf) correlates the appropriate attack verb to the model of the house auction described in chapter 1.

Figure 5.7: verbs related to the house auction

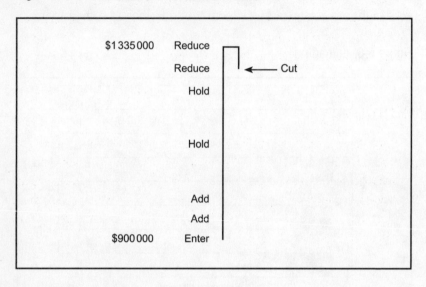

Processes rather than outcomes

Operation in the Peak Performance Zone is not alien to you. Reflect on how you drive. It is the integration of your physiology, emotions, thinking and doing in an unconscious, continuous and effective way. When you drive your car your actions just flow in a process that is beyond cognition. You are instantaneously responsive to the changes in the environment. You automatically do whatever is required each moment.

And you carry out each function or action without thinking of the overall journey. Nevertheless you know you will reach your destination. When you drive you don't admonish yourself because you have to brake or stop at a red light, or think you are clever just because you have overtaken a vehicle. Likewise in trading: at each moment you do what is required at that time, knowing that by doing so you are progressing to your destination. Overcome the temptation to gauge your performance by the outcome of this current action, rather than the overall journey. Trading is a process. Profit is the outcome.

Effective trading is a process just like driving. The outcome of the processes of trading linked to the flow of market traffic interpreted by your scenario will lead to profit overall. In other words: do the job properly and the outcome looks after itself.

Summary

Before you go for your trader's licence you will need to engage and practise the processes and skills of trading. That is to say you need to learn to drive before you get your driver's licence. Your trader's licence shows that you have built up the necessary skills base, or platform of processes, to then go on with it. The next chapter introduces you to your trader's L-plates.

L-plates: preparation for your trader's licence test

You wouldn't expect to just jump into the driver's seat of a car for the first time and pass a driving test out on the road. Yet most people seem to unrealistically expect to do this very thing in trading.

In fact you probably have a better chance of passing the driving test cold since you've had a lifetime of observation and familiarity with the processes of driving. Despite this, you prepared for your driving test by practice and repetition. You explored and implemented new skills. This led to your developing enough confidence to apply them on the road under different traffic conditions. To pass your test you had to display enough driving competence with an examiner watching you engage your range of skills with the unique route and traffic conditions that existed that day.

In the driving setting you realised the need for L-plates. Similarly you need the trader's equivalent of L-plates before you are ready to trade successfully. The role of this chapter is to prepare you for your test by helping you to develop your skills and confidence.

Becoming consciously competent

Let's examine the four stages of development in any field. You may have seen these before but it's worth considering them in the trading context. They are:

⇢ unconsciously incompetent

⇢ consciously incompetent

⇢ consciously competent

⇢ unconsciously competent.

SuperTraders function in the Peak Performance Zone, which surpasses the unconsciously competent stage. The hallmarks of working in the super-conscious state are vast experience, intuition, creativity, adaptability and guidance by principles arising from a deep understanding of the business.

On the other hand, those working at the other end of the scale in the unconsciously incompetent stage don't know what they don't know. In this category I'd include those who have developed some expertise in analysis—reading the road map—but don't realise that successful trading requires additional skills. These people dabble with trading a bit then move on in disillusionment. This is a pity because if they have the aptitude and passion there would be nothing stopping them from learning the appropriate skills and moving towards trading success.

Those in the consciously incompetent stage will commit to learning their job and go on to gain some experience in trading. They want to learn to trade properly. They are able to recognise recurring aspects of their situation and begin to apply general guidelines. However they find it difficult to prioritise and remain tentative, really only taking an arbitrary rather than a systematic approach. They find the going tough and will probably burn their accounts away if they cannot move on to the next stage.

Traders who are consciously competent have integrated their skills and experience in trading markets into a thoroughgoing perspective so that they are able to implement viable and successful trading scenarios. Competent traders know what is important and what is not. They have personalised their analytical techniques into an efficient personal trading style that projects high-quality scenarios. This affords them a feeling of enough mastery so that they can cope with most market situations. They know that following their rules and the unhesitating implementation of their scenario requirements is conducive to success. In short they have developed and know their edge. If they persist and constantly evaluate their work with the aim of improving their performance, they could move into the unconsciously competent arena and the Peak Performance Zone to experience the success that SuperTraders have.

To achieve your trader's licence you have to show that you are consciously competent at trading.

Essentially the process of learning a new skill involves learning the best-practice method and then simply repeating that over and over. To change or develop a new skill or process requires it to be forged into new networks in the brain. For the brain to secure a new process, it needs to be done over and over until it becomes automatic. This can take 1000 deliberate attempts. For example, to unlearn an inferior golf swing and relearn a better golf swing will take 1000 repetitions on the practice fairway before the better golf swing—essentially a new skill, although you already had an inferior version—is properly committed to memory.

Knowing about a skill isn't enough. It has to be practised. This is why learner drivers practise, practise, practise to install the correct skills to become competent.

It's a hallmark of professionals that they not only learn skills through initial practice but also keep working on them throughout their working life. Doctors are in medical practice. Professional golfers practise eight hours a day. Without disciplined and rigorous practice a ballet dancer would not be able to give the virtuoso performance on a Saturday night. One huge advantage that professional intraday traders have is that their skills are used repeatedly—that is, practised—throughout the trading day, every day.

What do you have to practise to establish the appropriate brain networks for successful trading? You will need to put into action the trading verbs, the development of high probability scenarios, and then integrate these two by putting the scenarios into practice.

Learner drivers carefully and deliberately take on the mantle of driver as they prepare for their licence. The reason we practise the actions and scenarios is so we can be profitable. In the same way I want you to 'act as if' you are a profitable trader and carefully and deliberately take on that mantle while you are learning.

The trading gymnasium: practise the verbs under instruction

The best way that I know of to learn new skills is through the guided practice of what I call the trading gymnasium.

The trading gymnasium is all about developing your proficiency with the defensive and attacking verbs. I have developed the idea from the learning model based on Cognitive Behavioural Therapy (a type of therapy based on the way we process information in the unconscious mind). At the same time as developing your proficiency, you will be systematically desensitised from negative feelings and emotions that distort your decision-making capacity and disrupt your trading.

The gym activities train you in skills that you can readily apply automatically and dispassionately in your trading in all market conditions, including high-pressure situations. You simply cannot crack when market pressure and the pace of your trading inevitably intensifies. At these times you need to be in complete control, and the trading gym helps you prepare for that.

Even at the highest level in sport the participants practise their basic skills before an event. At training before the grand final the coach will drill the team in the basic skills of passing, catching and tackling so that in the pressure of competition these skills will not fail the players. So too the trading gym provides the muscle, coordination and deftness for you to succeed in your trading business. It enables you to 'work out' before you enter the trading arena.

A word of warning, though: you do have to practise the essential trading skills. Remember unconsciously incompetent amateurs don't think they need to practise. To becoming consciously competent, you must practise.

Participate in the training. Have fun with it. My clients report that the supervised building of trading skills in the trading gym was a vitally important key in their growing ability to trade profits. They also experience liberation from fear and anxiety. Application of the skills has to become second nature to enable you to do your job.

Before we get started I want to discuss a couple of things. Firstly I am not an advocate of paper trading because it doesn't really commit you to the moment. It's like watching sport from the grandstand where it seems a lot easier than if you are on the field of play. Everybody is an expert in the grandstand. Secondly I recommend you use an internet-based electronic trading platform (for example the OANDA currency trading account) so that you are influenced only by your own ideas, and not those of a broker. By all means become familiar with the platform through its demonstration account, if it has one. Some trading platforms have a demonstration account whereby you are allocated 'funds' that you can practise your trading with. In fact you can use the demonstration account like a trading simulator in the same way commercial pilots spend mandatory time in the flight deck simulator.

Explore the platform's intricacies, potential and limitations. Become used to its leverage and the order type it allows before you allocate some money into a live trading account. You need to choose a platform that accepts small orders for $1 or $2 a point or pip for currency trades. I generally suggest that clients start off on an easy to operate currency or index trading account, even if you want to trade other instruments later. Remember the driving school car you learn in is probably not the same as the car you will drive when are licenced. It doesn't matter; the skills are transferable between trading instruments and time frames.

Your activity in the trading gym is not paper trading. You will be trading in real time with some real money. Even trading with a small amount of money requires focused commitment and makes the experience real. You are taking your car out on the back streets at first. The activities build up steadily from a small beginning. An analogy: at first you will be doing 'touch and goes' (landing and taking off) in a single engined Cessna, then doing planned flights and graduating eventually to jet aircraft and the jumbo jet.

With my clients I tailor the activities to suit their current situation. In this chapter I have set out activities that will progress you through the basic skills. My advice is to work through them all, but if you are fairly advanced as a trader then you will need to concentrate your efforts on the activities aimed at developing the skills you need now. If you are in the break-even rut, the attack verbs will be your priority. But remember, practising the basics will always pay off.

To begin with, place $1000 into your gym account. Select a platform that will suspend the account if your $1000 margin is extinguished. You will never lose more than $1000. Additionally, in the trading gym you will never risk your whole $1000 on any one trade, rather only a small fraction of it. What this means if that if you trade with a 20 point stop then at $1 a point you could have 50 losing trades before your $1000 would be eliminated. Very unlikely!

The aim is to build experience and develop skills, and you should be prepared to pay the price for this education. However overall if you follow these rules you will find that losses are small and manageable. Like some of my clients you may even make small profits by the application of the verbs, especially the attacking ones, as you work through the gym.

As you successfully build your skills you will smoothly and readily progress onto a bigger account. We are establishing a positive cycle. However if you can't manage $1000 under the controlled conditions of the gym then you should not proceed to increase your account. You aren't yet ready for your licence test.

In this exercise the aim is to practise trading skills independent of your analysis. Each of these examples, however, presents you with a small scenario. You have to visualise them to implement them.

The time period could be on a daily chart or down to a very short time frame, say five or 15 minutes. My recommendation for the gym is a 15 minute to one hour time period on a currency platform when the market is active. I make this recommendation because with a shorter time frame your results come quickly. The faster pace requires you to be well prepared and focused, and you experience more opportunity to practise.

Redo a particular task until you are at ease with it. Repetition is essential.

Here are some generic gym tasks for you to try. After the description of each task, I'll list the skills that this uses, and any further instructions you'll need.

Task: After the market opens buy a stock or currency. It doesn't matter which one. Three minutes later, sell your position to close it out.

Skill: Pulling the trigger (entry); trading agility.

Do this several times rapidly. Buy, sell, buy, sell, buy, sell, buy, sell. This task shows you how easy trading—that is, buying and selling—is.

Task: Buy a position and place a stop loss order of 2 per cent of your account or $20 under your entry price. This contingent order will automatically cut the trade if the stop is hit. If it hasn't been hit, close out before the end of the session. Remember to remove your contingent stop order if the platform you use doesn't automatically do this.

Skill: Setting and executing a financial stop (2 per cent); setting and executing a time stop (close out at the end of the period); trading agility.

Task: If this time period is an up on the previous one, plan to buy in the next period if the current high is breached. Plan to place your stop just under this period's close. Write your plan down or draw the scenario. If your platform allows, set a contingent entry and stop order that will automatically get you set.

Skill: Visualising a scenario; anticipation.

Task: If conditions are met in the new period implement your plan. You won't trade if the high of the former is not breached. Set a target to hold the trade for three periods only if not stopped out. Raise your stop each period under the close of the previous period if the market advances. On some trading platforms you can actually set the stop to trail automatically if you want to. That is, if the market advances 10 pips, the stop automatically advances 10 pips.

Skill: Implementation of a plan; technical entry and stop points; raising your stop; trade management with anticipated points; holding a position.

Task: Buy to open a position if yesterday's high has been breached with a stop just under yesterday's low. If the position moves in your favour keep raising your stop. When you are eventually stopped out, plan to buy back your position when the high of the next up period has been breached. Implement this plan when the conditions have been met. Again, place a stop loss just below the low of the previous period.

Skill: Being stopped out; paying rent; following your very next signal that is, reentry.

Task: Redo the previous task but on a longer time period. Set a suitable stop loss, financial or technical. (For example, 2 per cent or the low of the period before the high was breached.) Implement the plan if conditions are met. If the stop is not hit, don't close out. Raise the stop if the market advances.

Skill: Longer-term orientation; planning and implementation; setting initial and trailing stops. Hold.

Task: Target a position of 2 per cent or more above your initial entry price and buy another position of equal size if your target is reached. Raise your stop so that you do not lose on your total position. Apply a trailing stop if the market continues to move in your direction.

Skill: Scenario anticipation; holding with a winner; linear adding to a profitable position.

Task: Plan to add further if the position advances. Implement the plan if conditions are met. Raise your stop and execute it if it is hit.

Skill: Riding a winner; adding; coping with success.

Task: If not stopped out after five periods, close half the position out with a profit. If the next period is up, sell the remainder

Skill: Reduce; take; experiencing profit.

Task: Enter a long position (buy). Hold the position if it appreciates, while of course trailing your stop. But double your stop order so in effect as you are stopped out you will have automatically

entered a position in the opposite direction. Make sure you have
a cut point for this new position in the opposite direction as well.

Skill: Stop and reverse.

The permutations of the trading gymnasium are endless. Modelled
on the tasks above, you can design your own tasks to hone the skills
you need to develop. You can practise reducing after entry as well as
pyramiding and inverse pyramiding.

You certainly will need to practise the verbs by going short, that
is, selling to enter. You should perform each of the above gym tasks
with appropriate short scenarios and entries.

Handling one position at a time is enough at the start. However,
as you progress you can execute up to five different instruments at
any one time. If you want to add another to the five, then you will
close out the one position with the least momentum. At other times
you might be out of the market altogether if nothing suits.

Actually, when you have your trader's licence the maximum
number of positions you should hold from a psychological perspective
is 7 + or − 2. More than nine different positions lead to ambiguity
that can inhibit taking action.

The aim of the trading gymnasium is for you to experience and
develop confidence in the defensive and attacking verbs and your
capacity to apply them. Your skills emanate from thinking and doing
those things that enable you to manage risk and to be in control
whatever happens. This is the 'touch' whereby you are prepared to
pay your rent and make the most of your profitable opportunities.

Remember the aim of the trading gymnasium is to build your
skill proficiency so that you can perform under fire in your trading
business. To do this the skills need to be intrinsic and automatic. The
trading gymnasium enables you to develop confidence and trust in
your ability without paying expensive tuition fees.

The trading gym is valuable to you in the future. Before you trade
a new instrument or use a new trading platform in the future, design
some trading gymnasium tasks for yourself to make you familiar with
that market or platform. Learn to be agile with the instrument, both
on the long and short side, learn its pace and peculiarities, pay some
rent, work a winner, and load up.

The gym allows you to explore your trading style, your most suitable time horizon, enhance your patience and flexibility, and develop your management capacity.

Scenarios for the present moment

So far the trading gym has basically been about practising the defensive and attacking verbs skillfully. When you go for your driver's licence you will not be tested just on your ability to steer, indicate, brake, change gears, reverse or accelerate. You will be examined on how you use these skills to advantage while negotiating the traffic flow en route to your destination. You will have to brake at the stop signs, move round obstacles and cruise up to the speed limit when the traffic conditions allow. In short you will have to demonstrate that you can plan and skillfully implement a scenario that is appropriate to each moment in time.

Remember I said earlier that building a scenario was a whole-brain activity. You do it continuously when you drive; I want you learn to do it continuously when you trade. Now you are going to develop some scenarios and play them out in the trading gymnasium.

But first I want to introduce you to some psychology on scenarios. This quote comes from *Scientific American*, July 1998, page 120:

> In a simple experiment that requires a person to guess whether a light is going to appear at the top of a computer screen, humans perform inventively. The experimenter manipulates the stimulus so that the light appears on the top 80 per cent of the time but in random sequence. While it quickly becomes evident that the top button is being illuminated more often, people invariably try to figure out the entire pattern or sequence—and they deeply believe they can. Yet by adopting this strategy, they are correct only 68 per cent of the time. If they always pressed the top button, they would be correct 80 per cent of the time.
>
> Rats and other animals, on the other hand, are more likely to 'learn to maximise' and to press only the top button. It turns out the right hemisphere behaves in the same way; it does not try to

*interpret its experience and find deeper meaning. It continues to
only live in the thin moment of the present—and to be correct
80 per cent of the time. But the left, when it is asked to explain
why it is attempting to figure out the whole sequence, always
comes up with a theory however outlandish.*

To create a scenario you need to perceive at each moment where
the light is flashing, and just accept it. This is an intuitive capacity.
It needs to be legitimised and reinforced through, you guessed it,
practice in the trading gymnasium.

Here is a trading gym activity designed to release you from
left-brain analytical analysis hangups (if you have any).

Task: Fade your analysis. If your analysis shows buy, then open a
position by selling. The aim is to show you that your analysis
can be wrong and that your trading skill is paramount. If this
trade fails (that is, your analysis was right in the first place) then
scratch this trade and reverse it. That is, buy two positions now.
This closes your short and leaves you net long one position.
You have received confirmation from the market itself about
your trading action.

Skill: Detachment, flexibility, responding in the moment.

In reality the price in the market can only do three things: keep going
in the current direction, stay stationary or reverse direction.

Scenario planning involves being able to maintain your position
if there is no change in the scenario. But a scenario is always looking
forward to identify a meaningful change, which is an information
stimulus that requires a fresh response, a new action. The point is
that the scenario process enables you to be alert and ready for a fresh
action that is available to you before the change. The scenario is
always prepared for change; for implementation of a different attack
or defence verb. For example, in your car you might be cruising
along but you are ready to touch the brake pedal instantaneously if
ever any new information arises that requires it. It is the basis of the
old traders' saying: 'It's always best to dance near the exits.'

This is where the repertoire verbs come into operation. Scenario
stimulus: change in this moment. Scenario response: execute a new

verb. This enables you to act planfully in the present moment in accord with the market price flow. See the light flash: just do it. Let the left brain figure it out later.

The point is that the scenario prepares you in advance for the appropriate response because it is always looking forward for information that is anomalous to it: the light flash.

I do a lot of work helping assist traders to discern and act upon the light flash, the fresh stimulus. You don't have to be an expert at using intuition to receive your licence: but it will be an integral component of your development as you become a SuperTrader.

As humans we all have the capacity to do this. Almost all traders I come across have an intuitive reading of the market but deny it because of the almost universal false belief that trading is exclusively a left-brained activity. Have you heard the voice within that says things like: 'I should ... this price is retreating ... now is the time ...' and overridden it? No wonder the intuitive voice is only soft and non-assertive. It gets pushed aside so readily. But you can learn to value, trust and apply it for profit.

You intuitively implement scenarios automatically when you drive. How did you derive the confidence to do this? Because you practised them to pass your driver's licence test. In the same way the intuitive implementation of trading scenarios will need to be used to pass your trading licence test, enough at least to validate your competence.

The trading gym is an excellent place to start the process of scenario planning and implementation.

Figure 6.1 suggests a trading gym activity that is designed to enhance your capacity to respond immediately to a scenario change.

Task: The market has been moving down for a while against a general uptrend. If you detect a change in direction based on the shift of buying or selling, especially at an extreme, promptly open a position with what you think is the new direction.

Remember you may need to scratch this position quickly. Be alert. If the market justifies your first position then add two more positions and so on until the move is over. Then take immediately, and prepare for your next move of re-entry.

Figure 6.1: buy on first indication move down is over

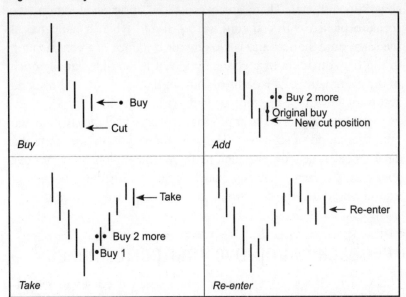

Skill: Scenario planning and execution. In this trade we are not only starting to employ your intuition as a legitimate tool for anticipation but also implementing appropriate verbs as the scenario develops.

Is there a role for the analytical left brain? Yes. When you drive it's useful to have a road map if you are in unfamiliar territory. You need to calculate whether you have enough fuel for the journey and to estimate your arrival time? However, it cannot usefully assist you to read the traffic flow moment by moment. In fact it's a distraction in reading the market.

In trading, the analytical left brain can assist you in determining the overall context and position of the market. Is it generally in up or down direction, or is it congested? How long has it been like this?

In short, the analytical brain enables you to put a general frame around your scenarios to read the market. For example, in a congestion or equilibrium market there is little movement in price to make money. (In traffic congestion you don't progress far either.) You would be flat. Your analysis will be looking for a break-out. Here is where your scenario comes into play, by determining what initial information would need to become evident in order to indicate the congestion is over. Then you execute the anticipated action, the scenario picked with a trading verb—if and when it happens. At the same time the scenario is looking for evidence of a confirmation in the new direction or a contradiction of it. You are equally open to the eventuality of a false break-out. In that case you will respond accordingly with the appropriate verb without hesitation.

The trading gym is the appropriate place to trial the creation and implementation of scenarios. The gym allows you the freedom and detachment to go 'out there' and really start to explore your intuitive ability as a trader. It enables you to engage with the processes of trading without being concerned so much about the outcome.

Feedback to improve your performance

The analytical side comes into its own when it comes to record-keeping and calculation of the benchmarks of your business; for example, hit rate or edge ratio. The purpose is not just to keep the analytical side busy. The analytical side has a major role to play in the collection and presentation of information that allows evaluation of your performance and feedback on which you can improve your business.

Of course you have to keep records of your trading activity. You need them to satisfy your tax obligations and to observe your performance.

Before you present for your trading licence test you need to have established a method to fulfill this function. Graphing the data (which is from the trading simulation in chapter 2) may help you interpret it: see figures 6.2 and 6.3.

In the final chapter I am going to show you how I use this data to evaluate and improve trading results.

Figure 6.2: the outcome of each trade in sequence

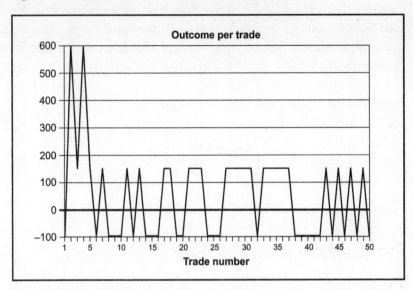

Figure 6.3: data re-sorted from worst to best result

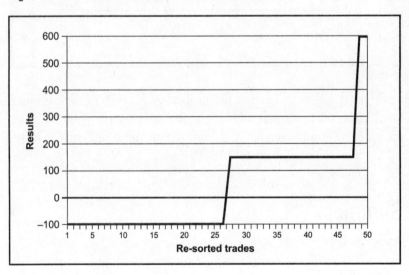

Another important way to examine the data is by drawing a continuous equity curve (see figure 6.4). This shows the progress of your business and the drawdowns, and you can relate the progressive trading outcomes to, for example, the type of market, or the impact of your star trades.

Figure 6.4: the equity curve for the data from the symbol simulation

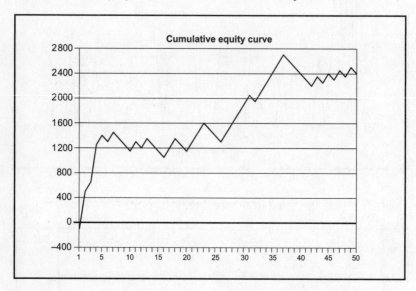

I said previously that loading up, properly done, is a money-spinner (see figure 6.5). Compare these figures to practise your skills at interpreting equity curves. Note: you record the results of a loaded-up trade as one trade when it has concluded.

Summary

Preparation for your licence to trade does involve good record-keeping for the smooth functioning and improvement of your business. It tracks the profits. But it is not the essence: you have to make the profits in the first place. This chapter has presented ways to practise the defensive and attacking trading verbs together with showing you how to integrate them into scenario construction and development. Having worked through the trading gym with your own tasks as well as the ones outlined in this chapter, you are ready to present for your licence to trade.

The next chapter outlines the theory and practical test for the award of your trader's licence. If you have the confidence to progress from your L-plates in order to display your trading competence, try it out.

Figure 6.5: equity curve for the moderate loading up

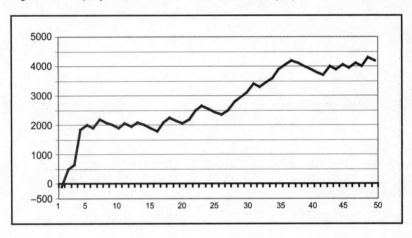

Your driving test: theory and practice

You've come this far: now it's time to present for your trading test.

Before you are certified as a competent vehicle driver you have to submit to and pass a theory and a practical test. You are required to demonstrate not only your knowledge of the road rules but also your ability to actually drive the car in real traffic. You aren't required to be a perfect driver; rather, an adequately competent one who then can go on with it.

These same criteria apply to your trader's licence test. Not only do you need to demonstrate your knowledge but also you have to demonstrate you can apply yourself to making a consistent profit by trading in financial markets.

In a similar way that your driver's licence test is competency-based, so too is your trader's licence test. You can keep repeating it until you get it.

The theory examination

Complete the following quiz. There are 10 questions to be answered, each on a scale of 1 to 10. The range goes from very strong disagreement (1) to complete agreement at (10).

Questions	Your score
1 I keep a journal of, and evaluate, all my trades.	
2 I never override my proactive scenario during a trade.	
3 A bad trade smells like rotten meat.	
4 The market is always right.	
5 Slippage and the spread are part of the game.	
6 It's better to put all your eggs in one basket, and watch the basket.	
7 Scaling into a big position is the way to go.	
8 I always implement stops when indicated.	
9 I think of the position, not the money.	
10 Trading is management, management and management.	
Total:	

The optimal score is 100, with 10 marks for each question. You need to achieve 85 out of 100 to proceed on to the practical component of your trader's licence evaluation. The quiz is based on information in the earlier chapters of the book, although some questions are purposely vague to stimulate your reflection about them.

If you didn't make 85 per cent, by all means reread sections in the book that you didn't score well on. However it should suffice to read the analysis guide below and then redo the quiz to achieve 85 per cent mastery.

Q. 1 I keep a journal of, and evaluate, all my trades.

Not only do you have to keep a record of your business activity but it is a mine of information for your improvement. Beginners want to ignore the losers. However, they have information for your development as much as the good winners. You are on your way to becoming professional in the business of profit management in financial markets—and part of the discipline is record-keeping, as well as continuously working for improvement through objective review and feedback from all you have done. In business you must know where you stand at all times. At the very least you must plot and use your equity curve as described in the last chapter.

Q. 2 I never override my proactive scenario during a trade.

You are mediating the market flow through your adaptive scenario. Your scenario is your forward vision. It enables you to adjust your position if there is a change. You may not feel like making the adjustment; you may prefer not to have to deal with it; you may not be able to give an analytical reason for it, but you do have to execute the scenario regardless.

Q. 3 A bad trade smells like rotten meat.

The small amount of capital you relinquish when you are stopped out is not a bad trade. Remember: it's your rent, overhead, your down-payment for the privilege of operating a highly lucrative business. But when you fail to implement your stop it is a loss. It stinks like rotten meat in your refrigerator. It's poisonous. Get rid of your bad trade immediately before it causes you harm and contaminates the other food. When the meat goes rotten in your refrigerator, it won't recover no matter how much you wish or wait for it to do so.

Q. 4 The market is always right.

Don't fight the market, or be frightened of it. You can never control it. You have to act on the action of the market, not your own desires or expectations of it. The aim is to develop scenarios that present you with high probability profit expectations by being in sync with the market.

Q. 5 Slippage and spread are part of the game.

These, together with broker commissions, are part of the cost of doing business. You should realise the worth of, and be grateful for, the opportunity that market-makers and jobbers give you by providing a liquid market that you can choose to trade when it suits you. In the same way you accept slippage that works in your favour, you should not resent those occasions when slippage works against you. It will happen. When it does, deal with it by taking the appropriate action, and then move on.

Q. 6 It's better to put all your eggs in one basket, and watch the basket.

Conventional wisdom says that diversification is the way to go. For investors it makes sense not to put all one's eggs in one basket. Remember diversification is a strategy to reduce risk. But as a trader interested in superior profits you want risk because the higher the risk, higher the return. You must become a skilful risk manager because that is what creates the profit. Recall, however, that the public perception of risk and a profit manager's perception of risk are quite different.

Your scenario at each moment of time is the way you watch the basket.

Q. 7 Scaling into a big position is the way to go.

This is the money management principle that we called 'loading up'. It enables us to have more money in our best ideas and less when the initial position doesn't work out. It is the way to make this business very profitable. Loading up is hard to do but it is an integral skill of SuperTraders.

Q. 8 I always implement stops when indicated.

The entry stop loss and trailing stop is your lifesaver. This rule is inviolate and automatic. It is the essence of sound defence to protect your capital. Don't alter your stop or hedge if it is hit. Just close this trade and go on to the next one.

The stop protects you financially and psychologically.

Q. 9 I think of the position, not the money.

Thinking of the money, whether when being stopped out, or when calculating how much your trade is making, reveals an ego bias that if fed will prevent superior returns in the future. During a trade you need to think about the scenario and the processes it requires you to follow. The outcome, the money, will take care of itself. Thinking of the money takes you out of the Peak Performance Zone. With good practice we expect profit. Don't be overawed when it eventuates.

Q. 10 Trading is management, management and management.

Management of the risk, your position, your account, and yourself is what brings home the bacon in trading. Another word for the execution of your trading scenario is management. It needs presence, discipline and non-attachment.

Now, before you go on to the practical test, I want you to do an inventory of your experience with the skills required to succeed.

Checklist of skill performance

On the checklist overleaf, tick off the skills you have executed in the trading gymnasium or in your trading experience. When you make the tick it indicates that you have performed the skill with competence.

If you cannot tick off a particular skill on the list, go back and practise it before you start your practical test. At this stage you need to be deliberate (consciously competent, in other words) at using these skills. After you secure your licence you will use them so much they will become second nature: you will do them without thinking.

Skill	Checked ✓
Enter	
Scratch	
Re-enter after scratching	
Cut	
Re-enter after cutting	
Hold a winner	
Add linearly to a winner at least two consecutive times	
Add in pyramid	
Add in an inverse pyramid at least once	
Reduce an entered position	
Reduce a profitable position	
Reversal entry	
Cut and reverse	
Take a profit	
Translated an analytical context into a high-probability scenario	
Executed a scenario for a continuation of direction	
Executed a scenario for a reversal	
Executed a scenario for break-out	
Executed a scenario based on an upcoming news event	
Prepared a spreadsheet for recording of results and equity curve	
Used feedback to improve your management skill	

Practical test: achieving the benchmarks

You will be awarded your licence to profit when you have proven that you can do just that: profit by trading in financial markets.

To demonstrate this you need to do around 50 consecutive trades and perform to a level that equates to a hit rate of around 50 per cent or better and an edge ratio of 2:1 or better. This is your trader's licence practical test.

Why 50 trades? When you go for your car driver's licence you are not asked to just take the car for a spin around the block. You are required to display your competence over a range of driving conditions for a protracted period. This gives both you and the public confidence in the licence. When you pass, you have demonstrated that you have worthily achieved the standard.

Likewise, you need to show your competence over the 50 trade standard. You will have hot and cold streaks—that is, is a run of winners and a run of losers; you probably will have both negative outliers to deal with and of course premium trades. You need to maintain your commitment and composure for a protracted period to have confidence in the licence.

To receive your licence you need to show you can drive in real market traffic. This is not for practice: although you might use the same trading platform as you did in the trading gymnasium, this is not a simulation. You are seriously displaying your competence as a profit manager.

Furthermore, you will now be able to manage up to nine positions simultaneously if you wish.

Like all tests, however, it's wise to set some qualifications.

The level of entry risk per trade should not exceed 2 per cent of your account to a maximum of $500 per trade. Even if your account size is above $25 000 you shouldn't exceed this $500 limit. When you have your licence you can move forward to a larger commitment. Indeed your licence shows that you are ready for and capable of doing so. If you can't handle a $500 risk competently, you won't be able to handle a $5000 risk.

Let's illustrate the process by working it through for a $20 000 trading account. The maximum entry risk is $400 for each trade over the 50 consecutive trades.

If, in the unlikely event every one of the 50 positions lost, it would be the end of the $20000. You'd have no capital left—and certainly no licence.

Perhaps in the 50 trades there could be a cold streak of 10 consecutive losers. The account would be down $4000. Still $16000 remains, or up to 40 trades left to identify and work the winners.

Similarly there could be a hot streak that results in your being $12000 ahead. In this case the entry risk would be maintained at $400 per trade.

So what can be expected if the licence benchmarks are achieved? Look at this example.

Hit rate = 50 per cent, edge ratio = 2:1
There would be 25 winners at $400 × 2 = $20000
There would be 25 losers at $400 = $10000
Profit = $10000

At the end of the 50 trades in the example, not only has the licence been achieved by securing the profit but also the account has risen to $30000 so entry risk may be increased accordingly for the next 50 trades. A virtuous cycle has been established.

Award of your licence

If you have secured a hit rate of 50 per cent or better and an edge ratio of 2:1 or better in your first 50 trades, congratulations! You have achieved your licence to profit by trading financial markets. Well done.

Fill out your name on the licence (see figure 7.1), photocopy it and frame it. It represents a significant point in your development as a profitable professional trader. By all means have a mini-celebration, but now you have proven your competence the invitation is really to go on with it in the future. This is what the final chapter of the book is all about.

Actually I require these benchmarks to be secured by all my clients, professional or otherwise, when I commence work with them. This creates a standard that forms a baseline from which we can work to direct and gauge improvement.

The most quickly a client has responded with his 50 completed trades was when he emailed his spreadsheet through to me at end of the next trading day. His hit rate was 54 per cent and his edge ratio 2.3:1.

Figure 7.1: your licence to trade

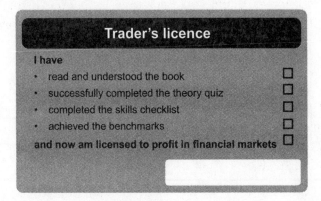

I am going to present you with data that is typical of most. A trader, Keith, works full-time, has a family with three small children, and operated his trading licence test around these factors. His entry risk level was capped at $500 per trade on a $25000 account. He could enter trades with less risk than this but never exceed it. Most trades he entered with a 'tester' much less than $500.

Keith accomplished these results over a seven-month period during which we worked together. His trading was conducted in the currency market. He never held more than one or two positions at any one time. Furthermore if there was no high probability trade indicated he waited flat, with no position, on the sideline.

Figure 7.2 (overleaf) shows his graphed results.

Here are some observations about his data. Trade 3 was a star trade. The longest winning streak was six trades (trades one to six), the longest losing streak was seven (trades 26 to 33).

Figure 7.3 (overleaf) shows the data re-sorted from worst outcome to best. It is important to note that, while there was some slippage on one trade, most of the loss trades did not amount to $500. This is an advantage of entering with a 'tester'. The average loss was around $150.

You will find that if you manage your trades from the start, most losses do not reach the maximum entry level of monetary risk.

Figure 7.2: profit or loss outcome for each of 46 trades in sequence

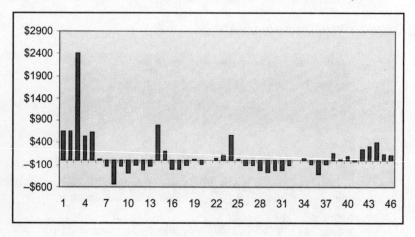

Figure 7.3: data re-sorted from worst outcome to best

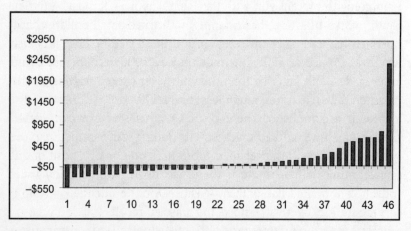

Looking at figure 7.3, would you award this individual his licence to profit by trading in financial markets? I certainly did. He achieved the benchmarks. His hit rate was 52 per cent and his edge ratio was 2.2:1. The profit he created was $4469 on his $25 000 account. Can he improve these results in the future? Certainly: that's what we are working on now.

What if you don't get your licence first time around?

The good news is that your licence test is competency-based. You can repeat it until you achieve it.

Not achieving your licence the first time around indicates that you have more work to do, more skills to practise in the trading gymnasium, that you need to work on better proactive scenario creation and execution, and generally that there's more for you to learn and change. As you know, if you keep doing the same thing you will receive the same result.

But don't be discouraged! Your results for the first 50 trades are very valuable whatever they are. From this tranche of trades you will be able to pin down where you need to focus to create the improvement required, as well as identifying what you do well.

You may not want to do the work however. One avenue you could take is to relinquish the quest of trading for profit. If you lack the passion and desire it will show up in only a half-hearted attempt anyway.

Profitable trading is only one of life's projects. There is nothing intrinsically special about being successful in the trading business. Go and find a project in which you can excel; be fully committed to and enjoy that. I had one frustrated client who in his futures trading account managed to lose $3500 each year over a period of years. I pointed out to him that he could join a high-calibre golf club for this amount and he might achieve more enjoyment. He took this to heart, gave trading away and is so pleased he did.

If you really want to achieve your trader's licence then you would benefit with some coaching assistance. At the very least you need to do the Traders' Personality and Behaviour Profile (made up of the Personality Needs Profile and DiSC Personal Profile, discussed in chapter 4) to make sure you are approaching the business in a style that suits your personality, together with the identification of your behavioural strengths and weaknesses.

If you practised the skills and used the trading gymnasium effectively then the issues preventing your success are probably deep-seated and to do with the interaction between your technique and psyche. At this point it might be advantageous to attend some professional workshops or do one-on-one work with a qualified coach. The real benefit for you here is that a professional coach can identify and remedy issues promptly and efficiently. This is personal and specialist work however, since we probably need to journey into your psyche: your conscious, unconscious and superconscious mind, to clarify and mend. Without this feedback and supervision you are left to your own devices that will entail trial and error, more frustration and dwindling capital and time.

Summary

The award of your vehicle driver's licence was a symbol of dedicated accomplishment and a new beginning in terms of the freedom to go whereever you like. However it was only the start of your driving career and the development of your driving skills. Similarly, the award of your trader's licence is a rite of passage for your future development as a SuperTrader.

Having obtained your licence, now that you are certified to trade for profit, let's turn to some of the challenges and opportunities that lie ahead for you.

The journey forward: from P-plates to peak performance

The achievement of your trader's licence is the conclusion of the first phase of your development as a profitable trader. It signifies your eligibility to grow and progress your trading business. It has established and confirmed the base from which you can reach for the consistent profits you desire.

However, your progress cannot be taken for granted. The award of your licence also indicates that work is just beginning. A medical graduate still has much to learn and much to do before she becomes a heart surgeon.

Here is a metaphor for what the attainment of your licence means. You have crossed the rope bridge over the divide from the losing and break-even zone, and now you are on the threshold of peak trading performance. You have just joined the top 10 per cent. Now you have to choose whether you want to retreat to the comfortable state of minimal success or whether you want to advance up the set of steps towards the professionalism and the SuperTrader status of the Peak Performance Zone.

Your trader's licence shows that you have discarded enough baggage and developed enough skills to cross the bridge. To journey up the steps requires continuous effort and the will to respond to the new challenges that inevitably arise as you move forward. Unfortunately there is no elevator! See figure 8.1.

Figure 8.1: peak performance

And one more very important thing: once you have crossed the bridge you have to cut it down so that there is no going back. You cannot hold on to the past and let go of it at the same time. Put in another way, you have to be committed to going forward with purpose on this exciting and liberating journey.

A note of caution

The award of your licence proves that you have enough mastery of the processes to trade profitably. It does not guarantee your success in the future. Now that you have your licence you have to build on these skills. The licence does not mean you can do away with them. In essence, you are on P-plates for a while.

Newly licensed drivers are the most likely to come into strife. Insurance premiums are much higher for young drivers because the statistics show they are the most accident-prone.

The driver's licence indicates an entry level of competency. New drivers are prone to underestimate the demands of driving in different and difficult road and traffic conditions. They are prone to take their licence for granted and overestimate their ability. Inexperience linked with a 'ten foot tall and bullet-proof' attitude is a recipe for trouble.

And exactly the same dangers await the newly licensed trader. To avoid trouble you have to be patiently committed to growing your skills and your experience in different and difficult market conditions. You have to become consistent.

In my coaching work I have noted a phenomenon that is so frequent that it is worth reporting and analysing. Many serious traders initially make a lot of money and then proceed to give their winnings back to the market, and then some. I'm not talking about those who dabble and have a lucky streak and then lose. I am talking about dedicated traders who over a period of months achieve superior returns. They make many thousands of dollars and then watch as the profit disappears, and yet they seem to be doing nothing differently.

Perversely, it is a 'riches to rags' story. It's an experience you don't want. It is a real possibility that you must guard against.

If it has happened to you then it is an experience that can sharpen your capacity to strive for consistent success in the future. Don't lose heart. Regard it as an initiation into the club of those who achieve consistent superior returns.

Knowing the cause can lead to the cure. The causes are numerous but we can categorise them under two headings: personal factors on the one hand and market factors on the other.

Personal factors

It would be easy to blame complacency. Perhaps you have taken your eye off the ball. You've achieved success and your emphasis on money management has slackened. The cure for this is to realise that continuous discipline and money management are the cornerstone of success and have to be applied assiduously and consistently every day, every moment of your trading life.

But applying discipline could be relevant in another personal dimension. Market participation is intense and personal management of the pressure and stresses involved can lead to burnout, even after six months. You must ensure that you retain balance in your life, building in relationship, recreation and renewal activities. If you feel stale, or that your passion for the job is declining, take a break. Opportunities abound in markets: it will still be there churning away when you come back.

The next set of personal factors is more serious because they can be hidden in your subconscious psychology. As a coach and therapist I look for answers to questions such as these: do you intrinsically believe that ongoing success in the markets is authentic, and if so do you feel deserving of achieving a superior income in this way? Are you self-sabotaging? Do you have other personality needs that aren't being met that even superior returns do not make up for? Because you have already achieved success we know that the issue is not a lack of aptitude. Rather we have to look at internal conflicts, needs satisfaction and other cognitive/behavioural issues that arise from initial success.

Market factors

It doesn't matter if over a period you have been brilliantly successful (or for that matter an abject failure), the market still wants your money. In fact the market is indifferent to your prior success: it just means that you now have more money that you can give back to it. How does the market achieve this? By transformation and what seems like duplicity, in an attempt to render your edge obsolete.

The thinking and ideas that gave you success will not endure as new market cycles develop. Many traders distill their thinking into technical analysis. But whether technical or fundamental, if your analysis gives you an edge now it doesn't imply that this will continue to happen in the future. In fact it probably won't: the familiar mantra that the market discounts successful analysis does come into play here.

You have three options:

⟶ Retain the analysis in the new market cycle and lose,

⟶ Stop trading until a future market cycle occurs in which the analysis is appropriate (which is unlikely).

⟶ Evolve and adapt the analysis to suit the new market conditions very early.

This is where proactive scenario development is so advantageous. This enables you to anticipate that the current market pattern will change eventually and that a fresh analytical procedure and scenarios will be necessary when this happens. It seems contradictory but nevertheless it's true that the time to be researching new analytical tools and scenarios for the future is when the current tools are working at their best.

Another market factor involves the question of leverage. It is entirely rational that as you become more successful your level of leverage increases. This implies that when the edge that created your success is at its most vulnerable, your leverage is also at its maximum. If your edge fails then your account is going to be hit hard, despite tight discipline. The problem is that if you are experiencing a run of success you will never know precisely when the run will be over. But you will know it's over when the plot of your equity curve starts to tank. This is when you must reduce your leverage until you regain your edge. You (or anyone) will not force the market. Throwing more money at it when your edge begins to fail is a recipe for disaster.

Your edge will fail when the majority starts to use it too. This will stimulate the market footprint to change and your edge will no longer be optimal. Your hit rate and equity will decline. Is this the time to fade your analysis? Possibly, you know your market counterparty is successful because you are not anymore. But it would be better to quickly figure out how to succeed in this next market phase knowing that this is your ongoing task as long as you want to trade over various market cycles into the future.

If you have just achieved your trader's licence you probably disbelieve that riches can rapidly turn into rags. But it is common enough and there is a chance that it will happen to you in your trading career. What a wonderful learning experience for a market player.

I'd sum it up thus: never take the market or your success for granted. Besides discipline and passion for the task the factor that will make you endure over a series of market cycles is flexible personal scenario creation responsive to market transformations.

While it seems obvious that coaching is necessary to get you started on the road to riches in markets, personal coaching is probably more important to enable your riches turn to greater riches rather than into rags. Although difficult to achieve, only 10 per cent do it consistently, trading longevity is possible and extremely rewarding for you both personally and financially.

A case study: how to improve

In this section I outline the processes and benefits that can be gained—both material and psychological—from a determined and deliberate effort to develop your trading into a reliable and efficient business. To illustrate this transformation I am using actual figures from a client, Jason, who trades short term currency futures. His only source of income is from his trading business. He has a wife who doesn't currently work, two small children and a mortgage. In other words, as the family breadwinner, he simply must succeed.

Figures 8.2 to 8.5 illustrate Jason's results. The bars are calibrated in thousands of dollars. It is for a $400 000 account with a maximum risk unit per trade of 1 per cent.

Firstly, I must reassure you that the data has not been polished or massaged in any way. The material is extracted directly from my working files. They represent a real snapshot of Jason's trading outcomes six months apart.

You will notice the considerable difference between the February and August data sets. Let's compare them using the trading business parameters of hit rate (wins as a percentage of total trades), edge ratio (return for the period divided by the outlay) and, of course, profit.

In February, Jason's hit rate was 37 per cent, the edge ratio was 1.37 and the profit was $19 900.

In August, his hit rate was 57 per cent, the edge ratio was 3.3 and the profit was $142 700.

Figure 8.2: the results of consecutive trades in a five-week period in February/March

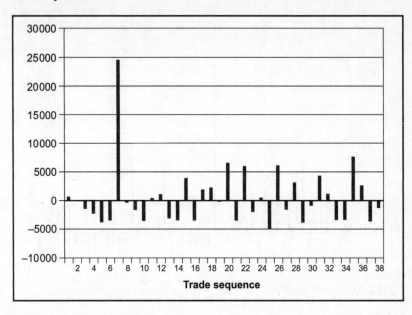

Figure 8.3: February/March data re-sorted from worst to best outcome

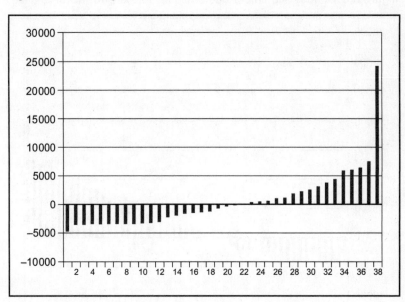

Figure 8.4: the results of consecutive trades in a five-week period in August/September

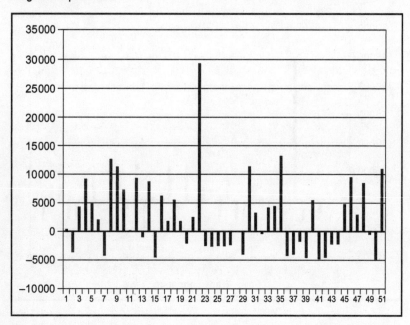

Figure 8.5: August/September outcomes re-sorted from worst to best

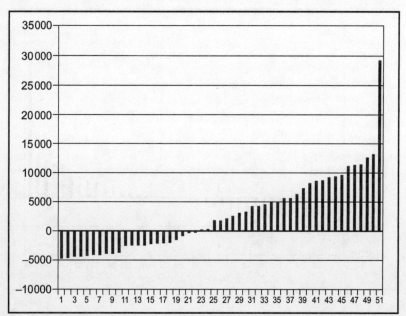

Why the concern over the February results? Figure 8.2 shows evidence of tight discipline in terms of risk control. Losses were rigorously stopped. A superficial view would say a $20 000 profit in a month is good. But when we examine it in detail it actually shows that the profit is heavily dependent on one good trade of $24 400. Take this out and a loss would have been made for the period. This is a profile of an account that prospers by attaining the occasional big win (or, in statistical terms, an 'outlier').

What is the change in the August figures? As well as obtaining the outlier, that is, the big $29 200 trade in August, Jason was able to secure a much better base for his trading business. Take out the one big trade and he still clears $113 500 for the month. This is the profile of an account that equates trading with a reliable and consistent business open to large returns.

How was the change brought about? We had already completed about 18 hours' worth of one-on-one work in the nine-month period prior to February. We identified Jason's personality traits, behavioural strengths and weaknesses, while building a professional coaching relationship based on mutual trust. We had reinforced the defensive rigor of Jason's approach, as well as extended his repertoire of trading skills. We started to work on viewing market opportunities in terms of probabilities instead of Jason's personal ability to predict the future. Furthermore, I worked with him to remove mental and emotional barriers and open up his potential using meditative relaxation and guided visualisation.

A crucial development occurred when we decided to meet weekly by phone for 15 to 20 minutes to discuss the previous week's specific trades. This allowed me to give Jason instant and objective feedback about his activities. This is one application of the methodology I use which considers the trader's outcomes that can be improved over time by using macro and micro feedback.

Specific examples of the type of issues we dealt with include the following.

→ *Impulsiveness.* Jason noted that he had a tendency to be impulsive in pre-empting rather than waiting patiently for scenario set-ups to materialise. A whole book could be written on impulsiveness but in this case it was related to Jason's deep-seated anxiety about action and wanting to do well. Unfortunately impulsiveness did not pay. The result was four or five trades a month that not only consumed money but also more importantly dissipated Jason's psychological capital as he was left to deal with self-recrimination and blame in their aftermath. The five trades on the extreme left of figure 8.3 were the impulsive ones. If we could eliminate the $20 000 loss associated with the five impulsive trades then the hit rate and edge ratio must go up. In August Jason did not make any impulsive trades.

⋯➔ *Upside scenario planning.* Jason was always disciplined in defensive risk-management. He told me that for him, controlling losses 'is just like brushing my teeth'. But we had work to do on the upside. Up until February he had a tendency to regard every trade as the potential star trade and if it didn't materialise—too bad! However, this left profit that was on the table drain away. Linked with active scenario planning based on the probability of likely outcomes (outliers are rare) Jason implemented an attacking strategy that enabled him to take most of what was on offer in each individual trade. The upshot of this was a significant improvement of the edge ratio. Note the plumpness of the returns on figure 8.4 compared with figure 8.2.

⋯➔ *Goal setting.* Over the years Jason had achieved a hit rate and edge ratio similar to those achieved in February. Yes he was profitable in the past (he made over $200 000 profit in the previous financial year) but his returns were variable and unpredictable (extract his best 10 trades for the year and his account would barely break even). He didn't intrinsically believe that he could better these figures and therefore hadn't consciously set out to improve these ratios. Our probability approach indicated that he should be achieving a hit rate of 55 per cent plus, and an edge ratio of 3. We set these figures as benchmarks that were realistically achievable. Of course a hit rate of 57 per cent and an edge ratio of 3.3 were achieved by August because Jason had worked deliberately and assiduously to accomplish this new goal. If we had never set these benchmarks as a goal to focus and measure his activity, he never would have achieved them. These are our minimum benchmarks forevermore.

···→ *Micro feedback.* We introduced the idea of 'maximum risk unit'. This is set at 1 per cent of capital. Risk per trade can never exceed this amount but it can be lower. Have a look at figure 8.3, and specifically the five consecutive trades starting with trade 23 (after the $29 200 bar). Previously, it had been a good trading period. We decided to cut risk per trade in half immediately after the $29 200 gain because we expected some reversion to the mean in terms of being closer to a losing streak. It paid off. If the risk was the usual $4000, then the account would have been $12 000 worse off. With the next win, trade 28, the maximum risk unit was reinstated. It is not wise to stop trading altogether after a winning or losing streak because you might miss the next outlier. If an outlier eventuated in the less than maximum risk period, then Jason could easily add back into it to achieve the benefit.

Other micro feedback strategies were implemented in accordance with the patterns that had previously existed in Jason's activity. We confronted and dealt with issues such as what to do when four or more losers in a row were experienced, how to distinguish 'outliers' from 'ordinary' trades, what to do in that week of the month that repeatedly showed a performance wane and even how to handle illnesses in the family that kept Jason from being active.

···→ *Peak Performance Zone.* It was also important to maintain and build Jason's presence and focus to keep him in the Peak Performance Zone. It would be wrong to underestimate the dedication and persistence that he applied in working towards consistent and efficient profitability.

Concurrently with dealing with feedback issues, we also capitalised on the psychological work we had already done and extended this base by in-depth, one-on-one 'inside work'. Jason and I worked together using discussion, meditation and active visualisation to stimulate his self-belief and confidence. In essence we worked with his 'will' to succeed. His success was well and truly secured in his psyche before it actually materialised.

What I have done with Jason and shown you here is the application of the Transformation to Peak Trading Performance Program that I employ to develop the edge of my professional trading clients. This particular program is not directed towards newcomers but is specifically designed to take traders from the award of their trader's licence forward, working to see who they may be if their potential as a professional trader is realised. You can see the psychological and intellectual demand required for the transformation as well as the benefits. With the right motivation and guidance, ordinary people can do extraordinary things.

The transformation Jason made between February and August is essentially one of personal growth. He was prepared to change and I was able to guide him. The process is ongoing. The success of the program is evident when you look at the data. Responding with more discipline, deliberation and diligence was pleasurable for him because while developing the necessary mental toughness, he was achieving his healthy desire to create a reliable and efficient business in trading. Now we are poised to really go on with it.

A model for progress

Once licensed, most drivers gain experience and develop their competence without major mishaps. By driving more they learn to become unconsciously competent and then super-conscious.

When you drive you function in the Peak Performance Zone. Your performance is reliable and consistent. You can master any challenge that confronts you.

The Peak Performance Zone in trading is reached in a similar way. Now that you have your licence you are on a mission to, if you choose, become more efficient and consistent, more reliable and flexible as a trader. By focusing on the deliberate improvement and practice of your ability to process the scenarios and skills required for success, you will achieve your outcome of consistent and growing profits.

Figure 8.6 shows a model for the development of your trading business now that you have obtained your licence.

Figure 8.6: expand your business franchise

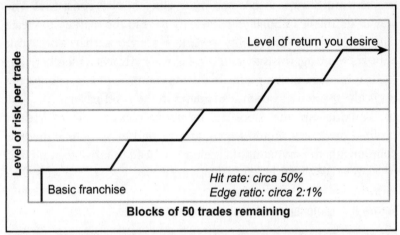

Once you have your licence you have to plan to grow in steps. It's no accident that this diagram looks similar to the steps in the model for professional growth presented at the beginning of the chapter.

On obtaining your licence you can't expect to be immediately an expert driver on the race track. It takes time, planning and effort to grow your trading business. If you achieved your licence with a risk of $400 per entry, don't immediately go to a $4000 entry risk, even if your trading account can afford it. You have to gradually become accustomed to the new psychological and management demands on you as you grow your business.

Now you have your basic business franchise, develop it in phases. Consolidate the next level with 50 trades achieving or bettering the benchmarks at this level. Go from $400 to $600 to $800 risk and so on. One of the problems that confronts any business is too rapid an expansion in the early phase.

Another way to approach the growth of your business is not to exceed an entry level of risk of more than 2 per cent of the account once your ability has been confirmed by your licence. On a $25 000 account with a $500 entry risk achieving a hit rate of 50 per cent and edge ratio of 2:1, the profit will be $12 500. The account has now risen to $37 500 so the new entry risk will be 2 per cent or $750.

You should always be looking for ways to improve your edge. While developing your business you should be looking for and implementing ways to become more efficient and consistent. The way to do this is to hone your capacity to read the market, to create and execute high-probability proactive scenarios that work your winners more aggressively and productively. Always remember your focus is on maximising profit. To do this you need to focus not on the unproductive trades but instead attend to the good payers.

Walking up the steps to greater achievement—to greater profit—obviously requires commitment and effort. There are two components to moving up the stairs. You need to move forward and upward at the same time (see figure 8.7).

Figure 8.7: dimensions of peak performance

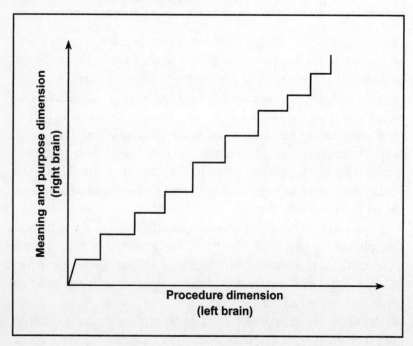

Your progress is not just a component of doing what you do now better. It is also a component of the meaning and purpose dimension. Furthermore, each dimension represents a particular brain function. The horizontal procedural axis shows left-brained analytical functions, while the vertical meaning and purpose axis indicates the right brain's creative/intuitive aspect.

To progress to the SuperTrader's Peak Performance Zone you need to combine both axes. The Zone is a response to whole-brained activity where the two dimensions are poised and balanced. You have learned to automatically be in the Zone with whole brain function when you drive a vehicle. Similarly, you can learn to be in the Zone when you trade.

In my experience people falter because their only focus is on the procedural axis. Their construction of meaning, their creative and intuitive side, is barred. On the other hand the creative and intuitive side needs to be grounded in viable, durable and efficient procedure for it to be useful.

Here is a small exercise to illustrate what I mean. Place your left-hand palm on the left-hand side of your forehead. In trading, most are taught and expect to succeed by using only the left forebrain. Now place your right-hand palm beside the left hand on the right side of your forehead. Now you can see that by using your whole brain you have doubled your brain's capacity to achieve. Ignoring half your brain means neglecting a powerful and resourceful asset to facilitate and contribute to your success.

Now place your hands on the back of your head. This is the part of your brain that you don't want to rely on in trading. It is the fight/flight area. It's meant for emergency human behaviour. This is where you default to when you react to sudden stress and surprise. Learned behaviour and experience enables you to accommodate with much more efficiency a suitable response to sudden change from your forebrain. This is so much more effective and desirable.

To be in the Peak Performance Zone requires you to operate with whole brain function in your forebrain. You do it when you drive your car to your destination. You can do it when you trade for superior profits.

Making the extraordinary ordinary

But will you do it? I have used the word 'will' deliberately here.

The 'will' is the conductor of the orchestra of your thoughts and behaviour. It coordinates your conscious activity and marshals your goals, meaning and intentions into the super-conscious Zone, if you let it. It harmonises your left and right brain functions. It is the will that coordinates your discipline, resilience and tenacity with the skills of scenario creation and execution leading to good outcomes. The good outcome is profit, and this must have meaning for you.

The achievement of your trader's licence shows that you can profit. Your task now is to go on so that you will profit consistently in the future. After you received your vehicle licence it was your will that enabled you to become the proficient driver that you are today.

Your great-great-grandparents would be amazed with your ability to work in the Peak Performance Zone while driving a car. Your capacity would appear heroic to them, yet it is ordinary to you.

When you move up the SuperTrader steps to the top 10 per cent, you will realise that the vocation is not extraordinary at all. When you work in the Peak Performance Zone creating a wonderful trading business for yourself and your family, it will seem ordinary. It won't seem special. It will seem natural. It's just what you do. Just like driving your car.

You will remember I stated in chapter 4 I stated that there is a problem with reading about market wizards and making them your hero. Yes, it is nice to have a model or models to show you that the journey is achievable. But the problem is that it can make the destination seem so remote. There is even a cultural tendency to sublimate or project one's own need for growth and achievement onto an 'out there' hero. It's the cottonwool the majority buffers themselves with to avoid the anxiety of becoming different and successful, and saves the need to take responsibility for their own journey.

Summary

In this book I have shown you how to secure your licence to profit by trading in financial markets. Now it's time, if it is your will, to really go on with it. Here is your opportunity to create your own future. In the end, you must become your own hero. Are you ready? Do you really want to? Then you will do it.

Index

If you found this book useful ...

... then you might like to know about other similar books published by John Wiley & Sons. For more information visit our website <www.johnwiley.com.au/trade>, or if you would like to be sent more details about other books in related areas please photocopy and return the completed coupon below to:

P/T info
John Wiley & Sons Australia, Ltd
Level 3, 2 Railway Parade
Camberwell Vic 3124

If you prefer you can reply via email to:
<aus_pt_info@johnwiley.com.au>.

Please send me information about books on the following areas of interest:

➤ sharemarket (Australian)

➤ sharemarket (global)

➤ property/real estate

➤ taxation and superannuation

➤ general business.

Name: ....

Address: ....

Email: ....

Please note that your details will not be added to any mailing list without your consent.